WHEN FAITH ENDURES

One Man's Courage in the Midst of War

WHEN FAITH ENDURES

One Man's Courage in the Midst of War

THE VAN NGUYEN AND DAVID LYNN HUGHES

Virgil N. Kovalenko, Research Consultant

Covenant Communications, Inc.

ALL PHOTOGRAPHS FROM VASAA ARCHIVES;
DONATED BY NAMED PHOTOGRAPHERS.

Cover image *Fishing Nets at Chau Doc, Vietnam* by Glen Allison © 2004 Photodisc Green/Getty Images.

Cover design copyrighted 2004 by Covenant Communications, Inc.

Published by Covenant Communications, Inc.
American Fork, Utah

Copyright © 2004 by The Van Nguyen and David Lynn Hughes
All rights reserved. No part of this book may be reproduced in any format or in any medium without the written permission of the publisher, Covenant Communications, Inc., P.O. Box 416, American Fork, UT 84003. This work is not an official publication of The Church of Jesus Christ of Latter-day Saints. The views expressed within this work are the sole responsibility of the author and do not necessarily represent the position of The Church of Jesus Christ of Latter-day Saints, Covenant Communications, Inc., or any other entity.

Printed in Canada
First Printing: September 2004

10 09 08 07 06 05 04   10 9 8 7 6 5 4 3 2 1

ISBN 1-59156-620-7

FOREWORD

My memories are very tender as I recall my visits to Vietnam during those trying times of what many Americans remember as an unpopular war. It was my special experience, representing The Church of Jesus Christ of Latter-day Saints, to have mingled and attended religious services with local civilians in Saigon. In subsequent seminars at the U.S. Army War College, I spoke with honest, favorable fervor about those with whom I worshipped in Vietnam.

I came to admire and love as my own brothers and sisters Saints like The Van Nguyen, our Saigon Branch president. Brother The was imprisoned for years in a reeducation camp because of his association with Americans. This story of his indomitable faith in the face of terrible defeats is remarkable, as is that of the Saigon Saints who were caught in that maelstrom of their country's collapse.

I am proud of all the LDS troops of the nations that served in Vietnam, as well as the Vietnamese Saints. They served with admirable unselfishness and courage. The legacy left in Vietnam by those men and women persisted and continued after the war. Their manifest devotion to the Lord and His kingdom is evidence enough of the quality of their service. I salute them and honor their wonderful service.

—Elder Marion D. Hanks
Emeritus General Authority

CONTENTS

Preface ix
1   The Funeral Service 1
2   The Formative Years 19
3   The Coming of the Gospel 35
4   In Defense of Liberty 53
5   The Distant Shores of Freedom 71
6   Departure of Military—Arrival of Missionaries 85
7   The Dream Unravels 111
8   And Great Was the Fall Thereof 139
9   The Reeducation of Tay 159
10 The Final Year at Mr. Five's 181
11 The Fresh Air of Freedom 199
12 Rebuilding Our Lives 223
Epilogue 239
Timeline of the Saigon Saints 255

PREFACE

by David Lynn Hughes

It's a miracle that I ever met the Saigon shepherd. It's a wonder that I ever cared to. For many years previous, I closed my mind to anything Vietnamese because someone Vietnamese, somewhere in Vietnam, killed my brother. I harbored anger toward God for not protecting him. Michael D. Hughes died July 14, 1969, at the age of twenty-four. Any concern I had for the Vietnamese died with him. Or so I thought. Then I met the Saigon shepherd. I learned of his trials, his faith, and his flock. He changed me, and God healed me. I so needed that.

I am the one who, at Michael's request, took him to the Salt Lake City Airport and dropped him off to wait by himself for the first leg of his flight to Vietnam. He had said his good-byes at a family farewell gathering the night before. There, in a sequestered, private room, he received a priesthood blessing for his protection under the hands of his five brothers, all of whom served in the military. His parents and three sisters looked on. Mother and Father had watched their sons leave for far-off assignments before, but there was something very ominous about this time. Michael would face actual combat. The whole family dreaded the thought, especially Mother. So somber was her mood, so foreboding her feeling, that we gave Michael, perhaps more for her comfort than his, a second priesthood blessing. It was a little more plaintive, a little more pleading, a little more urgent. Afterward, we rejoined the extended family in a fond farewell. It is understandable that after such a night, Michael did not want to go through another round of good-byes, anxiety, and tears at the airport the next morning.

Michael and I were among that portion of the prelottery baby boomers who were drafted at age nineteen unless poor health, college, or a mission deferred the call. I joined the U.S. Air Force at age eighteen, while Michael, two years older than I, deferred his military service to attend the University of Utah. He graduated in 1968 with a BS in microbiology and genetics and a high expectation of attending medical school. Unfortunately for him, U.S. involvement in the Vietnam War peaked in 1968. Over 550,000 U.S. troops were then deployed. His draft notice into the U.S. Army arrived shortly after his diploma. After basic training and advanced infantry training, Michael attended officer candidate school. Then he wavered. If he accepted a commission, an extra year of active duty was required. After much deliberation, he dropped out of OCS based on his determination to complete his army obligation and get back in school as soon as possible. The army immediately reassigned Michael to a combat unit and ordered him to Vietnam as a private first class.

So it was that I dropped him off at the airport that calm and beautiful morning near the end of May in 1969. His thick, dark hair was military short, a far cry from his college days; his blue eyes were not far from crying. A muscular and fat-free five foot eight and 165 pounds, he was a picture of health and strength. He was dressed smartly in his tan-colored army traveling uniform. Michael got out at the curb and hoisted his duffle bag over his broad shoulders. He was an accomplished athlete, very intelligent, and highly trained. I reasoned with my anxious self that he would make it; he'd come back alive. We exchanged waves as if he were going to Yellowstone Park for the weekend. "Take care of yourself, brother," I said as he turned and walked toward the terminal.

Forty-six days later, Michael was on patrol with a squad of fellow 82nd Airborne soldiers. Their assignment was to protect the perimeter around Saigon's Tan Son Nhut Air Base from enemy attacks. (At the same time, Brother The, also drafted into his country's army in the summer of 1968, was charged with protecting another area a few miles away.) Eight miles northwest of Saigon, Michael's squad came under a mortar attack in which he was hit and killed. Three days after the fact, the sad news reached my parents. Two army officers showed up at our front door early one morning and made the dreaded announcement: "We regret to inform you your son is dead." He died with honor, they assured, but no one heard a single word more.

An agonizing few days later, while the rest of the world celebrated the first man on the moon, Michael's body came home, gauze-covered, in a plastic bag, inside a simple military coffin. His body was unfit for viewing, so the army issued a large photograph to place on his closed casket as last respects were paid. An overflowing throng of mourners attended his funeral at the Sandy Second Ward chapel. We buried him in the Sandy, Utah, cemetery with full military honors. Seven precise army riflemen fired a twenty-one-gun salute. "Fire! Fire! Fire!" Michael's Vietnam veteran friends shuddered and flinched in unison at the sound of all three volleys. Our nation's flag draped his coffin. A lone bugler played taps. An honor guard ceremoniously removed the flag and carefully folded it into a triangular bundle of white stars on a blue background. The ranking officer presented the flag to our grieving mother "on behalf of a grateful nation." The Vietnam War came home to Pioneer Avenue.

After America had withdrawn its forces, like many Americans of my generation I tried to just forget the whole Vietnam experience. I could not. For fourteen years, I sought to make some sense out of the loss of my brother, the war, and my faith in priesthood blessings. I tried in vain to find *one good thing* about the war.

I did not know there were some 250 Vietnamese members and fifteen missionaries of The Church of Jesus Christ of Latter-day Saints in Vietnam in those few years preceding the fall of Saigon. It had not occurred to me that when the Lord said, "Go ye unto all nations," He could seriously be speaking of Vietnam too.

In answer to my belated prayers to overcome my bitterness and lack of understanding, I met The Van Nguyen (pronounced TAY VAN WIN), former president of the Saigon Branch of The Church of Jesus Christ of Latter-day Saints. We were introduced by a mutual friend, Virgil Kovalenko. Having served in Vietnam, Brother Kovalenko sensed my need for such a contact. In this he was correct because when I found President The, I also found my "one good thing."

By getting to know Brother The and other Vietnamese members, I gained a much deeper understanding of and gratitude for my basic freedoms and for those who protect them. I put my own so-called problems into proper perspective. Their example of sacrifice, of faith under fire, and of bearing incredible trials with humility, patience, and long-suffering are instructive and inspiring. Somehow, through learning of their

THE VAN NGUYEN, APRIL 1988
(photograph courtesy Leo Loving)

experiences, I replaced my bitterness with peace of mind, my chip-on-the-shoulder with forgiveness, my disdain with respect, and my hate with love.

The Saigon Saints provide a wonderful example of courage, endurance, faith, hope, and charity. Their leader, The Van Nguyen, the Saigon shepherd, was an ordinary man born in a war-torn country where life was difficult and opportunities limited. As a child, war, poverty, and disease shredded his life and family. As a young man of twenty-three, he found inner peace in the gospel of Jesus Christ. Even so, after he accepted the gospel, he was promptly thrust into the most difficult circumstances imaginable, and things just kept getting worse. That's when he advanced from ordinary to extraordinary.

He is a small, frail man, standing barely five feet tall and weighing ninety pounds. His skin and features are delicate. His temperament is mild. His quiet, respectful manner is patterned after a thousand years of Vietnamese culture. He doesn't complain about his trials; he rejoices in his blessings. Brother The is symbolic of what President Gordon B. Hinckley once said in a conference talk about finding "the silver thread, small but radiant with hope, shining through the dark tapestry of war" (see Conference Report, May 1968, 24).

The Van Nguyen is the man whose job it was to evacuate the Vietnamese Saints from Saigon even as it was falling to the communists. When outside help was cut off, he pressed on with full purpose and extraordinary effort to help his little flock. He is known as the Saigon shepherd. His is the scattered flock. His story is their story. Their story is his story. President The is amazed that he lived to tell about it. He feels that the time is now right when he can and must tell about it, or the opportunity to do so may be lost forever. I am honored to help him with such a worthy project.

In Vietnam, he was known as Nguyen Van The; in America, The Van Nguyen. (Please note that in the narrative "The" will be written as "Tay" for clarity. Vietnamese generally have three names of one syllable each. The family or surname is said first and the given name last. When he came to America, Brother The reversed his name to conform to the Anglo system of having the family name, Nguyen, come last.)

Brother The, of course, knows it is Christ who is the one true Shepherd, just as I know it is God who is the "one good thing" through whom all good things come.

The eventual successful outcome of most of the scattered flock is an example of how God works through His children to accomplish His purposes and to answer our most pressing prayers. It is also an example of how, when you are in the service of the least of these, your brethren, you really *are* in the service of your God. May Brother The's example of such service be as motivating and inspiring to you, the reader, as it has been to me, his friend.

CHAPTER 1

The Funeral Service

It is not often in The Church of Jesus Christ of Latter-day Saints that one gets to preside over the funeral of his own branch. Such was my unenviable task in Saigon, Vietnam, on Sunday, April 27, 1975, three days before the fall of Saigon. It was a beautiful, pleasant, clear day tucked neatly between the rainy season and the heat of summer. All who could attend, members and investigators alike, were there. We normally numbered just over two hundred Vietnamese members plus a dozen or more investigators ready for baptism. That day, duty called many of our military members to their posts. Many others, entire families, clamored at the airport seeking to find space on any aircraft leaving Saigon and dared not leave for the meeting. Commercial aircraft had ceased operations the week before. The scattering of the flock was already in progress.

It was hard to believe what was happening. The imminent fall of Saigon was simply unthinkable. Saigon had always been an oasis in the desert of war, an eye in the hurricane of blind fury, the king's X on the great battlefield of South Vietnam. Only last month, Saigon had been lulled by a peaceful dream from which it refused to awaken. The marketplaces were filled with green vegetables and raw meat. On Le Loi, Saigon's busiest boulevard, the pavement was piled high with peanuts for sale. Exotic aromas filled the air around Saigon's cathedral, where vendors in hot food stalls prepared their daily offerings. Every kind of vehicle filled the city's main thoroughfares. Up and down the boulevards, lined by huge tamarind trees, bells and horns and whistles kept time as darting, jerking, smoking bicycles, taxis, motorbikes, mini-jeeps, pedicabs, and small trucks delivered goods and passengers around the streets of Saigon.

Rather quickly, the atmosphere in the city changed. Everyday life became an awkward mixture of hope and rumor and fear. Saigon's citizens did not know for sure what was true, and they denied what seemed to be happening. False but optimistic reports that the U.S. Marines had landed at Da Nang and Cam Ranh were relayed by the Saigon press and happily received by the people. Then BBC news reports gave accurate but less desirable news, and the people again despaired.

Saigon newspapers were filled with notices which read "Xe ban" (Car for Sale) and "Nha ban" (House for Sale). Even though everything was priced far below its actual value, no one was buying. Fear drove Vietnamese women to fill barrels with dirt and sand to be used as roadblocks. Thousands of South Vietnamese troops strolled aimlessly through the city, searching for something to calm their fears. Somehow, everyone resisted the idea that Saigon would actually fall. We had strong hope that the city would be preserved against the heavy artillery that could be heard, muffled in the distance, but not so distant as before.

Members of the Saigon Branch had similar hopes. They had been gathered from the mass of humanity in Saigon and represented the firstfruits of the labors of the Lord in my homeland.

TYPICAL MARKET PLACE IN SAIGON, 1973
(photograph courtesy Lewis A. Hassell)

STREET VENDOR IN SAIGON, 1971
(photograph courtesy Virgil N. Kovalenko)

TROOPS IN THE STREETS OF SAIGON, 1968
(photograph courtesy Allen C. Bjergo)

SAIGON BRANCH MEETING PLACE, 1972
(photograph courtesy Alfred Hansen)

As branch president, I felt I was the watchman over the harvest. It was my stewardship to nurture, protect, and defend it. How overwhelming this noble cause seemed to be that day as I entered the gates of our chapel grounds and was immediately surrounded by so many nervous, questioning branch members.

"President Tay! President Tay!" they called anxiously. "What news do you have?" Their faces were a mixture of hope and frustration. As I continued toward the door, more questions were shouted out: "President Tay! Have the missionaries returned?" "Have the other members left yet?" "Without the Church, how will we be saved?" I shook their hands and patted their backs and looked into their faces. I had news, all right, but how would they take it? "Come inside," I said gently.

Sister Vy (pronounced VEE), the Relief Society president, took hold of my arm and asked anxiously, "What counsel do you have, President Tay? What shall I tell the sisters?" Sister Vy was an important part of the Saigon Branch. Her dark eyes seemed to look right through me as if she knew I had been holding something back. This small, delicate woman in traditional dress was descended from the Royal Family and was well educated. A former schoolteacher for many years, she assisted the missionaries in learning the Vietnamese language and customs. Most significant, she was the chief translator of the Book of Mormon. She was ever faithful in her callings.

"Come inside, Sister Vy," I said, motioning to the door of the chapel. "I will tell you everything I know after sacrament meeting." I appealed to everyone to remain calm. "Come inside, everyone; all of your questions will be answered."

The members of the Saigon Branch were my closest friends. I discussed many matters with them, but there were things concerning our possible evacuation that I was not permitted to discuss with anyone. The American embassy had warned me and the Hong Kong mission president, Jerry Wheat, not to talk about the proposed evacuation plan until it was officially in effect. There was great fear about the consequences of panic within the civilian population if they felt they were about to be abandoned. There was also fear that the frustrated South Vietnamese armed forces might turn on the American embassy personnel when they saw them leaving. We were thus instructed to say nothing of our plan until told otherwise. I was happy for everyone concerned when I had finally been released from this restriction. I planned to discuss the evacuation plan immediately after sacrament meeting.

The great cloud of fear covering the city also hovered over the Saigon Branch. It was well known to us that the communists took heavy reprisals against those who resisted their advance into Laos and Cambodia. We expected the same treatment. Saigon Branch members who associated freely with Americans, including LDS soldiers and LDS missionaries, feared they would be selected to receive an extra measure of punishment. Prudence dictated that we must leave. The question the Saigon Branch wanted answered was when and how this would be accomplished. As one city after another fell to the advancing communists from the North, time became our enemy. Bien Hoa, a major city just twenty miles northeast of Saigon and site of a major military base, was among those just captured. This startling news set off a new wave of panic in Saigon and in our little branch. It was under these desperate circumstances that we entered the Saigon Branch chapel to meet for the last time.

In those days the Saigon Branch met in a spacious rented French villa. It was part of the Chinese High School complex, where Vietnamese citizens of Chinese descent were taught.

The school owned dozens of villas surrounding the campus, which were rented mainly to American diplomats and civilian contractors living in Saigon. Because of the American withdrawal, many were vacant now. Our branch rented one of these large villas located on the main road between downtown Saigon and Cho-Lon (Chinatown). The grounds were beautifully landscaped with lush palm trees, towering tamarind trees, flowering shrubs, green grass, and colorful flowers.

From inside the branch chapel, the Vietnamese Saints who attended that clear, sunny day—about 125 souls—clearly heard approaching thunder. The thunder was from the rumble of heavy artillery and tanks, some defending, some assaulting the city. I could not withhold a brief, fleeting smile at the unbelievable irony of the moment. The same war that had provided the first seeds of the gospel in my Vietnam homeland was poised to ravage the field and scatter the harvest. I feared for all of us, but for me, the irony was also personal. I had been converted by the efforts of men who came to fight a war but found time to save souls. I helped military missionaries teach many of the current Vietnamese members and assisted the full-time missionaries by translating Church pamphlets into Vietnamese. I had joined this little flock in its early beginnings, and now I found myself about to preside over its demise.

Before the final sacrament meeting began, I sat at the front of the chapel and looked over the Saigon Saints and studied their faces. I saw the look of disappointment and fear in their eyes. Earlier, as I looked in my mirror, I had seen the same look in my own eyes. Sister Vy, the Relief Society president, took her place on the first row. Her troubled eyes betrayed her own sense of fear and inadequacy, a condition I shared in abundance.

I saw my friend Nguyen Cao Minh (pronounced WIN COW MIN) enter the chapel and quietly take a seat in my direct line of sight. He had once been president of this same branch until a military reassignment took him out of the branch area. Later he served in the Southern District presidency, which included the Saigon Branch. The district was dissolved when the Americans withdrew in 1973. Cao Minh was the first Vietnamese man to be ordained an elder in the Church and had remained steadfast and faithful ever since his baptism in 1963. A first lieutenant in the South Vietnamese Air Force, Cao Minh was still single, although in his forties. Perhaps Brother Cao Minh, I thought, and not I, should lead the branch in this crisis.

Brother Cao Minh visited with our friend Dr. Tran Van Nghia (pronounced KNEE-AH). Dr. Nghia was a young man who had just completed medical school a few months before and was immediately called to serve in the South Vietnamese Army. The army, the young doctor quickly diagnosed, was in very critical condition. Tran Hoang Nghia, a member I will call Brother Nghia to distinguish him from the doctor, was thirty-one and single. Both Nghias would have an influence on my future in the weeks to come.

As he joined me on the stand, I warmly embraced my second counselor, Le Van Kha (pronounced LAY VAN KAW). For a Vietnamese man, Brother Kha was large framed and powerfully built. He had a round face and wore eyeglasses that frequently slid down his broad, flat nose. His gentle, soft voice reflected his heart and temperament. A Protestant before being converted to Mormonism, Kha spoke eloquently of Christ and His Atonement. Widely respected for his honesty and wisdom, Kha lived in Saigon with his wife and four children. He earned his living as an office manager at Tu Du Maternity Hospital. Fifty years old at the time, Kha had been a member for four years. His family was not yet baptized. Sadly, the encircling

NGUYEN CAO MINH, SAIGON BRANCH, ABOUT 1966
(photograph courtesy William Haycock)

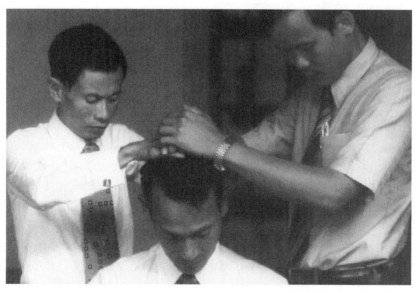

PRESIDENT TAY AND BROTHER NGHIA SETTING APART NGUYEN CAO MINH
(courtesy of The Van Nguyen)

war interrupted their gospel lessons. With his devotion to the Lord and his age and experience, perhaps, I thought, Brother Kha should be in charge.

My first counselor, Dang Thon Nhat, had successfully left Vietnam a few days before. A single young man, he left with his parents and his siblings when the opportunity to flee was offered to him by his father, who was not affiliated with the Church. My clerk, an American, was also gone. All of the American members of the branch were gone. The full-time missionaries were gone.

I wondered why I was left to myself to preside over the Saints in this time of crisis. I wondered why the Lord was permitting this national tragedy to occur. I could tell that many branch members wondered similar things. They sat in small groups and chatted among themselves, occasionally looking up to see if I was ready to begin the meeting and then returning to their chatter.

Brother Kha and I noticed that the Nguyen An Canh family was in attendance. Brother Canh, his wife, Mai, and their seven children were among the most recent converts, having been baptized only last month. The entire Doan Viet Lieu family of twelve, also baptized in March, stayed at the airport that day. They feared if they left for our meeting, they might not be able to return. Near Brother Canh was Brother Huyen, an honored veteran who lost his leg in the war and was not able to get around very well. Because of this, he was fearful, almost resigned, that he would be left behind. My wife had similar fears. She was sitting up front with our two young sons and our four-month-old baby daughter. I looked into my wife's eyes and smiled a nervous little smile. She held the baby close, her eyes pleading with me to save them. Nearby, her mother, sisters, and brothers sat waiting for someone to save them also. Some were members, some were not. There were many part-member families in our branch. We were still a work in progress when the progress ceased.

I heard loud explosions and mentally calculated their distance: too close for comfort. I worried about Brother Thach (pronounced TAUGHT), who was not present that day except in my heart. He was officially a member of the Saigon Branch, but he lived in Bien Hoa. Cao Minh and LDS American servicemen had taught him the gospel in 1970. When the Americans left, all the LDS military groups dissolved, and the Vietnamese members, if any, were assigned to the Saigon Branch. Brother Thach continued to go faithfully with his family to the deserted Bien Hoa Group chapel each Sunday. There, alone with his wife, Xuan, and their nine children, he blessed and passed the sacrament, gave a short lesson, and taught his children the gospel. Brother Thach was the first Vietnamese to baptize his own son. When Brother Thach completed Sunday services, he locked up the chapel and took his family home. With the fall of Bien Hoa, I feared greatly for Brother Thach and his family, as I had no knowledge of their whereabouts.

I observed carefully Brother Tran Van Long, a longtime member of the Saigon Branch, having been baptized in 1966. With Cao Minh, Long was among the first Vietnamese elders and had held leadership positions. Long had often expressed his worried feelings to me, frequently in excited bursts of agitated urgency. In Vietnamese society, it is against the natural order of things to have a younger person preside over his elders. Brother Long was among those who questioned the wisdom of having a thirty-two-year-old branch president. At this time of crisis, I tended to agree. Perhaps Brother Long, I thought, with his seniority in the Church, should lead us.

MAJOR JAMES HARRIS WITH NGUYEN NGOC HUONG (LEFT)
AND NGUYEN NGOC NGA, BIEN HOA, 1970
(photograph courtesy James M. Harris)

LOAN, DAUGHTER OF NGUYEN NGOC THACH, GIVES SUNDAY SCHOOL LESSON
TO FAMILY AT BIEN HOA CHAPEL, 1973
(photograph courtesy Alfred W. Hansen)

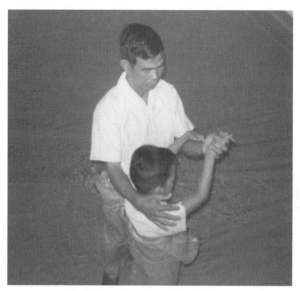

NGUYEN NGOC THACH, PRIEST, BAPTIZES HIS SON VU,
3 NOVEMBER 1971, BIEN HOA SWIMMING POOL
(photograph courtesy Virgil N. Kovalenko)

TRAN VAN LONG AND HIS FAMILY, JANUARY 1974 (TET CELEBRATION)
BACK, LEFT TO RIGHT: Tran Thi Ngoc Lan, Tran Thi Ngoc Anh, Nguyen Ngoc Dung, Tran Van Long
FRONT, LEFT TO RIGHT: Tran Thi Thanh Trang, Tran Thi Thanh Xuan, Tran Tri Dung

(photograph courtesy Tran Van Long)

Brother Dao Thanh Que and Colonel Nguyen Hai Chau were absent that day, but some of their family members sat anxiously before me, waiting to hear what measures were being taken to evacuate the Saigon Saints before the impending disaster. Brother Que was a high-ranking member of the government civil service who monitored the activities of South Vietnam's national assembly. Everyone knew, especially the families of high-ranking officers and officials, that the communists would not be kind to their vanquished enemies' leaders. In an added bit of irony, the missionaries chose to baptize Colonel Chau and his family on the previous Fourth of July so they could always remember they were baptized on America's birthday. Brother Que's family was baptized just last month, part of the accelerated efforts of the missionaries to do as much as they could as long as they could.

What a time to become a Mormon in Saigon! It was like arriving for a feast just as the hosts were clearing the tables. I studied the faces of each and every member and investigator present. Dozens of beautiful little children sat patiently by their worried parents. Teenagers on the brink of adulthood seemed to sense that their carefree days were over. Older members who had lived through many wars and occupations in their time were calm but very sad. Some members prayed, while others quietly wept. I wept inside but tried to appear confident outside. I was not. In this anxious moment, the Spirit of the Lord touched my heart and whispered that God knew of our troubles and that we were encircled in the arms of His love. All would be well in the Lord's own due time. The Spirit spoke amid the approaching thunder. All too soon, like Peter on the water, my faith faltered, and I sank back into my fears. Was it really the Spirit I felt, I wondered, or just my own desperate yearnings to be comforted? It was the Spirit. I recognized that comforting feeling and struggled to recapture it but could not. It was time to begin.

I rose to conduct the final sacrament meeting of the Saigon Branch before the fall of Saigon. There were no assigned speakers. It was not fast Sunday, but Brother Kha and I decided we needed spiritual strength from faithful testimonies. I felt the most appropriate opening song for this occasion was "Come, Come, Ye Saints." As we sang, I realized just how keenly we Saigon Saints came to know and *feel* the words of this great hymn.

> Gird up your loins; fresh courage take.
> Our God will never us forsake; . . .
> And should we die before our journey's through,
> Happy day! All is well!
> We then are free from toil and sorrow, too;
> With the just we shall dwell!
> But if our lives are spared again
> To see the Saints their rest obtain,
> Oh, how we'll make this chorus swell—
> All is well! All is well! (*Hymns,* no. 30)

We sang bravely, but all was not well in our troubled hearts. Few present knew very much about the early history of the Church. For them, the song could have been written especially for the Saigon Saints. If any Saints under heaven that day needed to take fresh courage, to trust in the Lord, and to feel that God would not forsake them, it was the Saints of Saigon. I feel justified to liken our feelings and fears to those of the early Saints. We didn't feel the wrath of our oppressors just yet, but we could hear them coming. We shuddered with each distant rumble that signaled our impending doom.

We had no desire to repeat history. A trail of tears and bloody footprints had often marked the trail the early Saints traveled to escape their enemies. They abandoned their homes and belongings and boldly, yet reluctantly, set out together to find a new place to dwell in peace. They simply wanted to worship God according to the teachings of the restored gospel. We in the Saigon Branch also saw our share of tears and of blood, but we doubted anyone could follow our trail to freedom. Scattered footprints leave no trail. Ours was a flock scattering in all directions, as if by ravening wolves.

The sacrament was blessed and passed amid tears and apprehension. I bore my testimony and turned the time over to the members. I had trouble concentrating on the meeting. I cannot recall these many years later all the words that were said, but I will never forget how I felt. My thoughts were as deep as the ocean, and the gulf between my needs and my abilities seemed as wide. My feeling of total dependence on the Lord was never greater. I felt inadequate to be in charge of the evacuation of the members of the Saigon Branch. Some members agreed that I was inadequate and rose to say so. Brother Cao Minh stood up and boldly reprimanded those who murmured against me and other Church leaders. He bore solemn testimony of the truthfulness of the Church and urged those present to trust in the Lord. I was thankful for his words of faith and support.

Another meeting was scheduled after sacrament meeting in which I was to reveal the evacuation plan and get a sustaining vote from the members on several of its points. My mind often raced ahead in anticipation of that meeting until it stopped in its tracks to sing the closing song. I remember the song very well: "God Be with You Till We Meet Again." Oh, how I sang and how I prayed! Tears filled my eyes and the eyes of everyone in the congregation. No one knew what our fate would be. We only knew that life as we knew it was over. We were saying good-bye to one another, and we knew it. We felt every word of the song and meant every sentiment expressed.

> God be with you till we meet again;
> By His counsels guide, uphold you;
> With His sheep securely fold you.
> God be with you till we meet again.
> Till we meet, till we meet,
> Till we meet at Jesus' feet, . . .
> God be with you till we meet again.
> (*Hymns,* no. 152)

The closing prayer was an urgent plea to Heavenly Father for mercy and deliverance even as our lives seemed to unravel before our eyes. With a subdued amen, the "funeral" concluded. It ended as many funerals do, with tears for our loss and a hope for reuniting at some time in the future. Still, it seemed cruel that the end came so soon, when our little branch was still in its infancy, with so much promise and so much yet to accomplish. The finality of it all was so unbelievable. I wondered, we all wondered, How could this happen? I trembled in fear for what might happen to us if we did not escape Saigon before it fell. In the privacy of my heart, I wept for my family and for myself, my home, my friends, my Church, my property, my station in life; all were in danger of being lost by one means or another.

The meeting to reveal the evacuation plan was next on the Sabbath agenda. After saying amen to the sacrament meeting closing prayer, the Saigon Branch members opened their eyes and through their tears looked steadfastly at me. No one spoke;

no one left; they just waited for me to speak. My inadequacies weighed heavily on my puny shoulders. I prayed for the strength to lead by the Spirit. I realized that what I said next was a matter of life or death to them. The evacuation plan was far from perfect, but it was all we had. I was expected to know all the answers, but my own mind was full of questions. How could this happen? Why was I left alone to lead the Saigon Branch? Why did the Lord gather us together just to be scattered?

With the passing of time, the Lord answered all of my questions to my complete satisfaction. I know He has a plan for all His children, including the Vietnamese people. I know His goodness and mercy will prevail over all opposition in His own due time.

I can look back from the present day on my own life and on the Saigon Branch and see the Lord's hand at every crossroads, every trial, and every triumph. I can say that now, but on April 27, 1975, I was at a loss for words. I had much faith but little understanding. I asked myself just how our beloved little branch and I had arrived at this point of crisis. Let us come back to this crossroads, the evacuation plan, later. First, we must go back into the past. The answers to my questions lie there.

CHAPTER 2

The Formative Years

My life and trials are typical of most Saigon Branch members. All of them led lives of constant struggle and felt the sting of death from war and disease within their own families, only to find inner peace in the gospel of Jesus Christ. In this sense, my story is their story, and their story is my story.

I was born in 1943 in Phu Nhuan village, five miles outside of Saigon, the largest city in Vietnam. I lived with my mother, father, and sister, Nguyen Thi Ba (pronounced WIN TEE BAH), in a small house on the outskirts of Saigon. My sister is five years older than I. Her name, Ba, signifies "number three" in Vietnamese. This name confused me until someone explained that my parents had had two other children, a boy and a girl. These siblings died, for reasons unknown to me, before I was born.

With my eyes closed and my imagination open, I can still picture my childhood home, just as it was, as if I were actually there. Come back with me. Look at my home as I see it in my mind. It is a "duplex" of sorts. It is one-half of a small, mud-wall house about thirty feet across the front and twenty-five feet deep on the sides. The drab gray walls are made from a mixture of mud and straw. A common wall twelve feet tall down the middle divides the home into two halves, each about fifteen feet wide. From both sides of the central wall extends a sloping, open wood framework supporting a roof of dried palm fronds. The ends of the roof are attached to shorter mud walls, perhaps seven feet high, on the sides and back of the home. The front of the home is a combination of mud wall and wood. The front door has an open-air window lined with wooden bars. Between the pitch of the roof and the top of the front and back walls is more open space for ventilation. Bamboo shades are lifted or lowered to allow more or less airflow and light, depending on the degree of protection needed to shield our little family from the elements. It is a humble home, but it is typical of others in the surrounding neighborhood.

Look inside. The mud walls have no windows. Look up and see the roof of palms. There are scattered beams of sunlight poking through. Rain finds its way through the same holes. The floor is bare dirt, smooth and hard. There is no plumbing, no electricity, and no telephone. The toilet is outside behind the house. A hanging bamboo curtain divides my father and stepmother's sleeping area from the rest of the house. They have a manufactured bed made of bamboo. The bed Ba and I sleep in is made of long wood planks laid side by side across supports that resemble carpenter sawhorses on each end. Mats cover the planks. In the kitchen area is a stove made of hardened earth and mud. The rounded stove is flat on top. The opening in the front is for burning wood to make heat. There is also room for a pot. A stack of dead branches and wood scraps lies next to the stove. Cooking pots for rice and vegetables sit on a wood plank by the stove. A kerosene lamp, filled and ready to provide light, is on the small table. Across the room there is another wood plank lined with several large pots containing water drawn from the community well with a rope and bucket and then carried home. The water is for drinking, for cooking, and for bathing. Beside one bucket is a water dipper made from half a coconut shell with a long handle attached. Using a bucket of water and this dipper, we bathe ourselves in the corner. With my eyes closed, I can picture it all.

How well I remember my home! It was a place to sleep, a place to eat, a place of shelter, and a place to be a family. I loved that home.

My mother's brother lived in the other section of our "duplex" home with his wife. They had no children. My uncle worked for the Buddhist temple, which owned extensive tracts of land in our area. He worked at the Buddhist cemetery. He prepared graves and maintained the grounds. He sometimes worked on the Buddhist temple farm. The priests were kind and allowed him to cultivate and grow food for himself and our family on the vacant areas within the Buddhist property. Sufficient food proved to be a great blessing for us. The lack of available food was the first thing on most people's minds when they arose in the morning and when they went to bed at night.

When I was born in 1943, World War II raged in the islands of the Pacific and throughout the western world. The Vietnamese were calloused by war. The Chinese ruled the land for centuries. The French came to Vietnam in the 1600s, beginning with French Catholic missionaries and followed by French settlers. In 1861 the French military seized Saigon. They eventually conquered all of Vietnam and signed a treaty with its people in 1883. Along with Cambodia and Laos, they formed a federation constituting French Indochina. They remained in power until Germany conquered France in World War II. The Japanese took over my country shortly before my birth. After World War II, the French returned and attempted to regain control. A Vietnamese Army leader from the north, Ho Chi Minh, led a Vietnamese communist group that drove out the French in 1954. Afterward the United Nations politically divided the country, with a demilitarized zone separating North and South Vietnam. The industrialized but agriculturally poor communists from the North then focused their efforts on taking over the peaceful agricultural society of South Vietnam. The North called it a war of liberation and reunification. The South called it a war of aggression and fought to expel the invaders and to retain their freedoms. The United Nations, led by the United States, resolved to intervene in the conflict and try to prevent South Vietnam's fall to the communists. The United States supported the South's defensive war effort over the next two decades until they too withdrew in 1973. Two years later, the North conquered the South and reunited the country under the banner of communist rule.

From the day of my birth to the day I left Vietnam nearly forty years later, I never beheld a single day of true peace or freedom in my Vietnamese homeland.

Even as my country struggled for survival, I struggled in my personal life. I frequently lost. My mother died when I was two years old. I was told she accidentally fell and struck her head on something hard, rendering her unconscious. She lay for several days without skilled medical attention and died from a brain hemorrhage. She was twenty-nine years old. I do not remember my mother, but I take comfort in knowing she loved me. I was nurtured at her breast and learned to crawl and walk and speak my first words under her watchful eye. She could not be a big part of my life, but I know I was a big part of hers at the time she died. I have gazed fondly at her photograph and have often longed to feel her embrace and hear her voice.

My father remarried and life went on. My memories of my father are scant but deeply imbedded. I remember his loving smile, his calloused and often paint-stained hands, and his tireless efforts to provide our family with the necessities of life. My father worked in the city of Saigon. He was a professional automobile painter, a foreman in charge of about ten other painters. He worked very hard to provide for our family.

Late one night when I was seven years old, my stepmother, my sister, and I were awakened by very loud gunshots. We lived near the police station, but these shots seemed even closer. Ba and I scrambled for cover under our long-plank bed. Stepmother, with no room under her bed, quickly joined us under ours. We stayed on the floor under our bed of planks for about an hour to avoid any stray bullets. After the commotion outside subsided, we climbed back into our beds and went back to sleep. In the morning, my uncle, as was his custom, arose very early and went to a nearby little food shack and drank his morning coffee. There he heard the news that my father had been shot and killed by the police during the night.

Father had worked late in the paint shop and stopped after work at a bar for some drinks. He delayed his return beyond the established curfew, which was around eleven o'clock at night. The French were in control of the police department in those days and established the curfew to curtail crime and mischief. They also feared the infiltration of communists from the North, who were then seeking to expel the French from Vietnam. After curfew, the policy of the police was to shoot first and ask questions later. For whatever reason, my father was killed by mistake at age thirty-seven.

My uncle hurried back to our house to tell us the news. My sister and I could not be consoled in our grief, while my stepmother seemed more angry than hurt. We all went together to the hospital morgue where the authorities had taken my father. We found him laid out in a room with two other corpses. At the incredible sight of my dead father, I trembled and cried furiously as any terrified child would. My twelve-year-old sister, Ba, also cried and mourned loudly, but she managed in her grief to hug me and try to console me, or at least provide me the comfort of her embrace. The other two bodies were dead from several days before, and the heavy, nauseating stench that filled the warm, stuffy room was as unbearable as it was indescribable. Two men came and took the other bodies away for burial. Still, the odor was overpowering. The smell of death, I learned as a young boy of seven, is worse than any smell on earth. The odor is so offensive that when God created vultures, He mercifully withheld their sense of smell. As for me, I could not bear to look upon my father one moment longer under such odious circumstances.

My uncle told me to wait outside in front of the hospital. I went out to the welcome abundance of fresh air and sat down alone on the curb, where I mourned the death of my father and pondered my own sad fate. I waited for what seemed to be about two hours. At one point, the men assigned to bury the two corpses saw me alone and crying. They came over and sat beside me, perhaps to comfort me. In this they failed. The smell of the corpses permeated their clothing and hair and skin to the extent that they smelled nearly as bad. When they observed my disgust and discomfort, they departed from me.

Within days after my father died, my stepmother left our house and took everything we owned with her. She decided Ba and I were not her problem. It was hard for me to first be orphaned and then be abandoned by my stepmother, the only mother I ever knew. I could not understand why these terrible things were happening. I remember my pain and guilt when I realized the shots we heard that night killed my father and how we all just went back to sleep. Maybe, I thought, we could have helped or comforted him.

In my culture, with no one else available, it fell upon my mother's brother to look after my sister and me when my father died. My uncle was a good man, and we loved him. He and his wife willingly took us in and treated us with all the kind regard and tender care of loving parents. I should mention that my uncle sold his half of the house, and he and his wife moved in with Ba and me. We were thus able to continue our schooling and continue living in a familiar area. Uncle resumed his work at the Buddhist cemetery and farm, and we had sufficient to eat. But perhaps the added burden of caring for us was too much. He was a frail man, and maintaining life was difficult. His health slowly declined.

My uncle developed sores on his lower legs that gradually increased in size and severity. Soon he developed deep lesions, which grew larger as time went on. His flesh dissolved into a runny, stinky mess that exposed his lower leg bones to open view. The sores gradually extended above his knees and into his thighs. He no longer worked. Doctors came but could do nothing for him. He had a cancer or advanced diabetes, which was beyond their ability to treat. Weak and worn out, he died when I was eleven. My uncle's wife continued to live with us, but due to her poor health, most of the time it was we who cared for her. She did what she could to help and always provided the wisdom of her years and maternal love worthy of any real mother. All too soon she fell ill with some disease she could not overcome. We had no more money for doctors or medicine but did our best to make her comfortable. Within one year after my uncle died, his wife joined him in the silent relief of the grave. My mother's mother, our grandmother, then came to live with us. Within a year, from natural causes, she also died.

Woe was me! I was not yet a teenager, but I had lost both parents, a brother and sister I never knew, my uncle and his wife, and my grandmother. If this was not enough, my stepmother had abandoned me. Frightening thoughts constantly revisited my mind: Ba and I would run out of people to take care of us. What were we to do? Why was my life like this? Was it my fault? Would I be the next to die? Would I ever know happiness?

After my uncle, aunt, and grandmother died, although some extended family helped occasionally, it was ultimately up to my sister and me to provide for ourselves. Most of my father's family resided in the central part of Vietnam, and some lived in the North. None were available to help. My mother's family, from the Saigon area, was nearly depleted. My fear of being left alone in the world was intense and terrifying. My inner turmoil was sometimes so great that my stomach felt as if it had been kicked. I often trembled when I was awake and aware of my circumstances. I often cried in my sleep when my dreams provided me with even more imagined trials. It was difficult enough for adults to maintain a living in such a poor country. I wondered how I, a mere child, and my sister, not yet a woman, could ever survive. I feared with all my being that we could not. I felt as if we were somehow destined to have a lowly and miserable existence, that fate was against us.

Mutually burdened by the weight of our gloom, my sister and I vowed to take care of one another to the end. The time for crying was over. The time for hard work was at hand. We reasoned together and devised a plan for our survival. Because of my uncle's farm experience, my sister and I were somewhat familiar with the business of selling produce. My uncle's privileges on the Buddhist farm were not extended to us, but by using such wits as we had, we imagined a possible path to our salvation. First, we sold our portion of the house we lived in and paid to have another smaller and even more humble dwelling built for us just a few feet away from our former home. With the money left over, we went into the produce business.

My sister and I arose before sunrise each morning. We walked together four miles to the Phu Nhuan village farmers' market. We arrived at five thirty in the morning, before the market opened, to buy fresh produce from the local farmers, some of whom were acquainted with our circumstances. We bought the best vegetables we could and took them to our rented "slot," or stall, in the marketplace. The large, open marketplace, about the size and shape of a football field, had a covered area in the center for fresh meat and chicken. The covered center was surrounded with hundreds of stalls, where fruits, vegetables, and other products were sold by individual vendors. The arrangement was similar to a huge flea market in America. It was one of dozens of similar markets situated in and around Saigon, a city of over two million people. Feeding them was a daily, all-consuming event in which we played a tiny role. We sold our vegetables for a profit, and each day we would buy a few more vegetables, the next day a few more than that. We gradually increased our daily inventory until our stall was fully stocked to start each day. We settled into a daily routine, arising in the dark, walking the four miles to the market, then, when the market closed after lunch, returning home, weary from our long day, but proud to carry home the money we earned. We held out enough money to maintain our lives and buy more vegetables. We saved the rest. The cycle continued day after day. My sister was a good negotiator and obtained a fair price for our produce. From her example and by observing others, I developed some business sense of my own. In this manner, we worked side by side for our survival and honored our vow to help each other.

Once we were established in the business, we devised other means of earning money. In the afternoon, when the market closed, we came home with leftover vegetables and cooked them. I took them outside and sold them on the street for snacks or quick meals. I sold cooked sweet potatoes, cooked bananas, and taro root. I also sold cassava (a large, starchy root) and various kinds of fruit.

When we were comfortable with the idea, we decided to further expand our little business. We hired our aunt, my mother's oldest sister, to help us at the marketplace. She lived near the market. We supplied her with live chickens in the morning to sell in the covered area of the market. We obtained these chickens from nearby farms or along the way to the Phu Nhuan marketplace. I carried the chickens to the marketplace. With two or three chickens in each hand, legs tied, beaks pecking, and wings flapping, this provided an eventful walk to the market. It was also very hard work and tiresome to the arms of a small boy. The chickens scratched and pecked all along the way.

I did not like the "chicken division" of our little enterprise. Once the chickens were at the market, my aunt boiled water, slit the chickens' throats, soaked the chickens in the water, and plucked their feathers. The chickens were then sold fresh to the people in the marketplace. Sometimes I helped pluck the feathers, which I hated. Handfuls of hot, wet, stinky feathers yanked from the skins of the chickens ended up all over my skin, my clothes, and in my hair. At the end of the process, I too needed to be plucked. On most "chicken days" I was happy to help Ba with the vegetables at our produce stall and leave the chickens to Auntie. Our aunt was in her fifties but was not

RURAL VILLAGE NEAR SAIGON TYPICAL OF THE AREA WHERE TAY GREW UP
(photograph courtesy Allen C. Bjergo)

ON THE WAY TO MARKET, 1971
(photograph courtesy Virgil N. Kovalenko)

in good health. After a year or so of selling chickens at the market, she was no longer able to work and came to live with us. Then, as you might guess, she died.

The most profitable time for our business was during Tet, the Lunar New Year festival held in late January or early February, depending on the cycles of the moon. For several thousand years, this has been a time of great celebration, feasting, and increased hope for happiness, prosperity, and peace. During Tet, we sold double or triple the usual amount of vegetables. We also got a seasonal boost in income by selling flowers for Tet. We contracted with farmers two or three months in advance for the crop of a specific portion of their flower field. Whether the flower crop failed or flourished, the price was set. We could only hope for a good crop. The farmers continued to care for the flowers until just before Tet, when we harvested the flowers from our section and took them to the market. We sold mainly orange marigolds, red gladiolas, and red poppies to the people. During Tet, business surged, just as it does during the Christmas season in America.

Ba and I operated our little business together for two or three years. By then, my sister had matured into a beautiful young woman of sufficient age to marry. She did so. Her new husband moved in with us. This arrangement and the extra income of her husband somewhat relieved our burdens. Ba's marriage gave me an opportunity to make a change for the better while my sister and her husband attended to the business. I had another plan: to finish my education.

Even after their military departed, the French operated the school system in Vietnam. It was very efficient and thorough. I had finished five years of elementary schooling before my uncle died. Then I had to quit school to work in our produce business. After my sister married, I went to the paint shop where my father had worked and asked for a job. I was then about fourteen years old. Because of my father's former position and because he was remembered in their hearts, they kindly hired me as an apprentice painter. I got all the menial and less-desirable duties in the paint shop. I quickly determined that the work of painting cars was too difficult and my health too delicate to continue indefinitely on a full-time basis. The dust from sanding old paint and the fumes from applying new paint greatly irritated my lungs. Sometimes my lungs hurt, and sometimes I was short of breath. At all times, I was skinny and weak. With sister Ba's approval, I decided to paint cars by day and continue my schooling at night so I could prepare for more suitable employment. Thus motivated, I worked as needed and studied continuously. I finished the normal seven years of remaining studies in just four years.

This was no small feat. I had one glaring deficiency my first year back in school. I was not good at math, and at the end of the year I was at the bottom of my class in that subject. I could not work with fractions or algebra, because I was not taught these things in my village school. I took it upon myself to improve during the summer break between school years. I went to used book dealers in Saigon and bought all the math books I could find. I studied very hard on my own and learned to work out math problems using the books I bought. When I came back to school, I was the first in my class to raise my hand and solve the math problems presented by the instructor. I finished that year at the top of my class in math. This gave me confidence and demonstrated to me, as had the produce business, that hard work led to improvement in life. My weakness became my strength. It was a good lesson to learn.

School, under the French system, was very demanding, particularly the last three years of curriculum. These years are divided into two parts of what we know as the baccalaureate. Batteries of difficult tests are administered at three important times. The first test is to qualify for acceptance to the three-year program; the second, at the conclusion of the first two years of the baccalaureate; and the third, at the end of the last year of baccalaureate. If you passed the final test, you graduated with the equivalent of a junior college education. If you failed the final test on any subject of any year's curriculum, you repeated the entire course of study for that year and then retook the tests. Along the way, once you passed any test, and not a day sooner, you were advanced to the next level.

My courses of study included history, literature, chemistry, physics, math, algebra, geometry, geography, biology, English, and French. The tests were never multiple choice or fill in the blank. The tests were always comprehensive compositions or calculations to demonstrate your grasp of the subject. It was very difficult. How great then was my joy and relief to complete even the first half of my baccalaureate!

After completing the first two of the final three years of studies, I left the work of painting cars behind me and began to tutor others. My successful completion of the first two years of studies was recognized as the credentials to teach. I financed my remaining education by tutoring younger children in their homes. Eventually, I opened a "school" in our home to teach the neighborhood children according to their needs. Most children wished to improve their skills in math, English, or French. Both English and French were very desirable to learn because of the extent of French and American influence on South Vietnam's economy. Vietnamese citizens with a foreign language skill, especially English, had greater access to good jobs and a better life. Because of this, my tutoring services were in great demand. Tutoring had the added benefit of improving my own language skills.

After successful completion of the second part of my baccalaureate, I was prepared to look for a job with a future. I found a good job at the Hawaiian Dredging Company as a blueprint operator. I also printed maps and other documents. I enjoyed my work. I was finally in a position to provide a living for myself and also help my sister. Even better, I did so from the comfort of my desk rather than tax my weak and weary body by doing strenuous labor. Sadly, my employment there ended when their projects were completed. Discouraged, I set out to find a new job.

First, I had to contend with the draft. Communist forces from North Vietnam were still attempting to overthrow the government of South Vietnam. When I was twenty-one, as required by law, and with the war against the North still raging in the countryside, I registered for the draft. The draft board physical exam determined that my health was substandard and that I was unsuitable for military service. It was the first time I ever rejoiced in being a small, frail, and sickly boy. However, because of my education and experience, I was placed on inactive status as a reserve army officer. In the event they drafted me later, I knew I would be sent to train as an officer. I felt fortunate when I received my deferment, and the war no longer seemed a direct threat. With this behind me, or so I thought, I renewed my efforts to find steady employment.

I heard someone say that the United States Agency for International Development (USAID) was hiring interpreters. Although I had not yet heard of the Mormon Church, even then the Lord directed my path, preparing me for future work in the Church as well as providing a means of future escape from my difficulties. I took the qualifying test at USAID and passed with high marks. I did much better, in fact, than my actual skills would have predicted. Again, the Lord blessed me.

I was pleased to be hired and started a new career as an interpreter of conversation and translator of written documents.

My economic conditions improved drastically when I worked for the American dredging company and then USAID. I earned money beyond my needs and saved the excess diligently. When we had sufficient funds, Ba and I once again sold our home and built another house, only this time we improved our living conditions. We constructed our new home with cement walls and tile floors and louvered windows, all of which our other homes lacked. Most wonderful of all improvements, our new home had electricity. Electric lights and the ability to utilize simple appliances like fans and a radio or phonograph made life seem grand. We still lacked indoor plumbing, but we had clean water nearby and carried it to our home, which was located right next to our previous homes. Like our childhood home, it was built as a duplex. I lived on one side, and Ba and her husband lived on the other.

Our long ordeal of hard work and difficult trials finally bore fruit. For the first time in my life, I felt good about myself and my prospects for the future. I had reached my lofty goal of more education, better employment, and improved living conditions. What more could I ask? My life, for once, seemed to be in order. I had earned the rare feeling of self-satisfaction. Within this peaceful eye of the storming war around me, three more years passed quickly by. I was by no means looking for a change in my life, but change came looking for me.

CHAPTER 3

The Coming of the Gospel

In the spring of 1966, when I passed through Saigon one night, I noticed an American, an airman in the U.S. Air Force, who was having trouble with his motorbike. It was a small bike, a Bridgestone 50 cc, typical of those used all over Vietnam. His attempts to communicate with a Vietnamese repairman brought little success. I walked over and offered to help. I know now that my Heavenly Father, who no doubt watched over me through my childhood trials and perhaps even joined me in my tears, arranged this set of circumstances so I could be introduced to the gospel. Oblivious to His omniscient ways, I unknowingly cooperated as the seed was sown.

I was twenty-three years old at the time. I had practiced my high school English on Americans for several years while working at the Hawaiian Dredging Company in Saigon and was currently translating English at USAID, so I felt pretty comfortable as an interpreter. When I offered my help to this American stranger, I was only doing my duty, as is anyone who is in a position to help another.

"May I be of assistance?" I asked. I watched the American's face beam with relief.

"You sure can, buddy," he answered. "This conversation is going nowhere, and neither is my bike. My name is Roy Moore," he said, extending his big friendly hand, which totally engulfed my own. "I am based at Tan Son Nhut," he added, referring to the huge joint Vietnamese-American military air base in Saigon.

To Vietnamese, all Americans seem tall and fair. Such was the case with this airman. He was bigger and friendlier than most Americans I had met, however. I liked him immediately and introduced myself. "I am Nguyen Van Tay. You call me Tay. It is simple for Americans to say."

"I really appreciate your help, Tay," Airman Moore said politely as I assisted him in the matter of the motorbike. In the middle of my services, he surprised me by saying suddenly, "Say, Tay, what do you know about the Mormon Church?"

"I know nothing," I confessed, somewhat confused at the turn in our conversation. "I am a Buddhist."

"Well, I will visit you, and we'll talk about it sometime," he said in a matter-of-fact manner. "What is your address?"

We completed our business with the repairman and were left to ourselves for a few moments. As we parted, I found myself exchanging addresses with this young man. I was not so much interested with his religion as with cultivating a new friendship. When I did not hear from him as expected within a few weeks' time, I sent him a letter to remind him of our meeting. Still, I heard nothing in reply, and I considered the matter ended. Finally, two months later, I received a letter. Airman Moore apologized that he had been sent away on temporary duty elsewhere and had just returned to find my letter. The next thing I knew, Airman Moore and another LDS serviceman visited me at my home. They taught me about their religion as we met together eight times over the next two months. Airman Moore came each time but sometimes brought different companions with him. They used a flannel board and picture cutouts to teach me about Heavenly Father and Jesus Christ, Joseph Smith, the plan of salvation, the Word of Wisdom, tithing, and other doctrines of the Church. Although they were not official LDS missionaries, Airman Moore and his companions taught me by the Spirit, and I felt stirrings within my soul that there was much good in their teachings.

One might think that a Buddhist would be hard to convert to Mormonism. In my case, it wasn't as difficult as one might imagine. I already prayed for blessings to make my life better, only I prayed in the Buddhist manner to my ancestors. I believed that they still lived in some other sphere of existence and that they still had concern for me and my problems in life. I prayed to them to offer what assistance they could to help me. To pray to Heavenly Father instead was a comfortable thing for me to do. I had no difficulty believing in the eternal nature of families and readily accepted the notion that families could be sealed together. This was perfectly logical and appropriate to me. As to the Word of Wisdom, by prior choice I did not smoke or drink coffee. Airman Moore asked me to give up alcohol and tea, both of which I used socially but could easily refrain from using if I so chose.

Every Sunday, Airman Moore came to my house to get me on his motorbike and took me to church meetings at the Saigon Branch. These were not held in a church but in the private residence of an American civil service employee within a civilian compound area. I was fellowshipped and made to feel wanted. Their little group consisted of mainly American serviceman, about twenty-five, sprinkled with a few, maybe ten, Vietnamese members. This little cluster of Vietnamese Saints represented the firstfruits of the gospel in Vietnam. Church services were held twice on Sunday. In the morning, we gathered at the house for priesthood, an abbreviated form of Relief Society for the half-dozen females, and Sunday School. We had no Primary in those days. We used the living room as a chapel and the kitchen and bedrooms as classrooms. In the afternoon, sacrament meeting was held in the living room.

This time of learning the gospel was a good experience for me. I was led to ponder things I had previously never considered in depth. Where did I come from? Why was I here? Where was I going after I died? It was both mentally stimulating and socially enjoyable to exercise my mind in this manner. The gospel discussions with my itinerant missionaries opened both my mind and my heart. Attending church services awakened in me a desire to belong to such a meaningful group of useful and good people.

I did have problems with the law of tithing. It seemed unreasonable to me to ask 10 percent of the incomes of Saints so poor. I was better off than most Vietnamese, but even I did not think I should be expected to make so great a sacrifice. I struggled greatly with this requirement.

When I finished the discussions and read some of the Book of Mormon in English, I was ready to pray in earnest about the things that I had been taught. One night, I knelt in sincere prayer and asked my Heavenly Father if what I was taught was true, and then I listened for His answer. A warm, loving feeling washed over me, and my mind seemed to open with clarity. I understood what I had been taught. The Spirit told me with certainty that the Church was true, that the Book of Mormon was true, and that the gospel path was the true way to be united with my parents and loved ones. I knew then that the LDS Church offered the better path to follow. I finally accepted the law of tithing. Exerting more obedience than faith, I tested the principle. It is difficult to explain the economy of the Lord, but in defiance of worldly logic, income really is somehow expanded and expenses really are somehow lessened. I found over time that my 90 percent served me as well as or better than my 100 percent had previously.

Even before I believed in tithing, I believed in Jesus Christ and His gospel. Although I knew little about the temple, I was especially interested in the concept of an eternal family where my association with my father and mother, whose deaths I grieved with such anguish in my childhood, could be renewed and continued in the next life. Also, the brother and sister I never knew could be part of an eternal family. The gospel also offered hope for all those poor souls lost to war and disease whose lives seemed without joy or meaning. I was thankful that Heavenly Father did not forget all those who had not heard the gospel or partaken of its blessings. It seemed fitting that they too would be given their opportunity for happiness in the spirit world and beyond. The plan of salvation, even in its most basic precepts as taught to me, was a wonderful plan. I believed it and embraced it. I had not previously considered myself religious in any formal way, but now my mind was suddenly riveted on the things of God and heaven.

But all was not well at home. My sister, Ba, whom I loved and respected greatly, did not share my interest in this new faith. My investigations into Mormonism caused some discord in our home. She was hurt to think I would go against the faith of our parents. Although I was not a devout Buddhist, Buddhism and ancestor worship was the traditional belief of my family and my culture. Most Vietnamese practiced one of the eastern religions, such as Confucianism, Taoism, Buddhism, Hinduism, or some combination of these. Others, about 15 percent, were Christians. Christianity was first brought to Vietnam by French Catholic missionaries beginning in the 1600s, and by the 1970s tens of thousands of Vietnamese belonged to various Christian sects. For Ba, Buddhism alone was the faith of our family. Our entire culture teaches the principles of honesty and integrity and honor for one's parents and elders. Ba's opinion was therefore of great importance to me. We had relied on each other through all our trials and vowed always to help one another. Because we did, our lives were so much better now, notwithstanding disputations over religion. In her eyes, to seek another path was to dishonor our parents and their teachings. Furthermore, she reasoned, we were good people already. To her, a change in religions was simply unnecessary. I was ready for baptism but not quite ready to offend Ba. My love and respect for her remained the biggest obstacle to my joining the Church.

Because I was the eldest surviving son, the duty fell on me to burn incense at the altar in performance of ancestor worship rites. It is a tradition taken most seriously. For me to consider another religion, especially one that forbids such practices, was hard for my sister and extended family to understand. As a result of the missionary discussions, I pictured myself at another altar, within the Lord's house, where I would honor my parents by participating in the sealing ordinances for my departed loved ones. With no temple within thousands of miles and no means to travel to one, this may have seemed an empty and hopeless dream. I believed it nevertheless. The more I studied, the more necessary baptism seemed to me. That was when I prayed to Heavenly Father about this peculiar new faith and asked if it was true and received the peaceful assurance within my heart that it was. I was unfamiliar with the Spirit at that time, but I could feel a warmth and assurance within me such as I had never known before. I also believed that Heavenly Father actually knew me and that my life had a purpose and that, perhaps, He had a work for me to do. This new kind of feeling was evidence enough for me. I greatly desired baptism. I inwardly looked forward to the mighty change in my life that I expected baptism would bring.

As much as I loved my sister, I could not honor her wishes above those of my Savior. My decision to be baptized caused my sister to become bitter and full of shame. She still loved me but looked upon me as a fool who had lost his way and wandered from the prescribed path. She resented how my "foolishness" would reflect badly on her in our community. I, in turn, felt a great sorrow in my heart for her, because I knew I had chosen the better road to follow. I chose to cast my lot with the little band of about a dozen Vietnamese Saints in Saigon and to put my trust in the Lord Jesus Christ.

On September 3, 1966, after four months of attending LDS Church meetings, I was baptized. We used a borrowed baptismal font in a Baptist church for the occasion. It was truly the early days of the Church in Vietnam, especially for the Vietnamese members. About half of the branch, six Vietnamese and a dozen Americans, attended my baptism. I did not feel anything miraculous occur as I came out of the water, but I knew that I had taken an important and necessary step. On Sunday, the gift of the Holy Ghost was conferred upon me. I had felt the influence of this Spirit when I prayed about whether to join the Church. I also believe the Lord had touched my mind and influenced important decisions I made before I joined the Church even though I had no knowledge of His plans for me. Now, I welcomed with gladness the

SAIGON BRANCH CHAPEL, 1972
(photograph courtesy Alfred W. Hansen)

BAPTISMAL FONT BORROWED FROM BAPTIST CHURCH, SAIGON, 1968
(photograph courtesy William M. Haycock)

prospect of the Spirit's constant companionship. Little did I know how greatly I would come to depend on this special gift. Airman Moore bestowed another gift I came to depend on. When he left to go home to America, he kindly gave me his motorbike. I used it for my primary transportation from that day until I left Vietnam.

In my new little branch, I was welcomed as a fellow citizen of the gospel by my new American friends and by others from my homeland who had embraced the gospel. I became fast friends with Cao Minh, the first Vietnamese man ordained to the Melchizedek Priesthood, and later with Sister Vy, who was baptized August 25, 1967.

I spoke with them separately and learned the story of their conversions. Besides being Vietnamese, our one common denominator was that we all spoke English well enough to be translators. Indeed, my first Church calling was to assist in the translation of Church brochures into English. Cao Minh and Sister Vy, immediately after their baptisms, were likewise soon engaged in preparing the gospel to be taught to our Vietnamese brothers and sisters in their own language. It is most interesting to see how the Lord's hand always stands ready to set events in motion whereby He can extend His invitation to "come, follow me." As in my own case, wherein I met Airman Moore with his broken motorbike, Cao Minh and Sister Vy each had a story to tell of how they were plucked from the masses and planted with the Saints. What some might call coincidence, we know is the hand of God. The Lord had a work for us to do.

Cao Minh was an officer in the Vietnamese Air Force. He had been sent to Biloxi, Mississippi, for training with the U.S. military. LDS servicemen he "just happened" to meet there introduced him to the gospel. He accepted the gospel and was baptized in America on August 14, 1963. He returned to Vietnam after his training and joined with an LDS servicemen's group as one of the first few Vietnamese members. (Two Vietnamese women taught by LDS servicemen at Tan Son Nhut were baptized in February 1963. They are believed to be the first Vietnamese members of the Church. Their names are Duong Thuy Van and Nguyen Thi Thuy.)

Cao Minh, who had read the Book of Mormon in English and had a testimony of its truthfulness, was very desirous of making the book available in Vietnamese. Elder Gordon B. Hinckley, then an Apostle, came to visit LDS servicemen groups in 1965. Cao Minh earnestly pleaded with Elder Hinckley at that time to have the Book of Mormon translated into Vietnamese. Elder Hinckley asked if he was willing to do the translation. Brother Cao Minh, though willing, knew his military duties would hinder the progress and drag out the work, so he declined. Instead, he reviewed and edited the work of others. He took a few newly translated pages with him on each of his military assignments, made his comments and suggestions, and exchanged them for more pages upon his return.

Sister Cong Ton Nu Tuong-Vy is an elect lady. The title *Cong* in her name means "countess," for she is descended from Vietnamese royalty, but she is known simply as Sister Vy. She was introduced to the gospel in an unusual way. Around 1966 Elder Hinckley authorized the raising of funds for a possible future chapel for the Saigon Branch. The branch president at the time, Robert J. Lewis, who was also an architect, decided to look for possible places to build. He wanted to know who was the most honest real estate agent in Saigon and inquired of a trusted Vietnamese friend. Sister Vy's name was given. Brother Lewis went to see her at her office, which also provided travel services. He explained what he was looking for, and she

SISTER VY, SAIGON BRANCH RELIEF SOCIETY PRESIDENT, 1970
(photograph courtesy Clinton H. Gillmore)

NGUYEN CAO MINH, SAIGON, 1965
(photograph courtesy Ray Wood)

drove him around Saigon to show him properties that might meet his needs. In the process, she asked him about the church he represented and what he believed. She was sincerely interested and asked to know more. She, in effect, asked him the "golden questions." Brother Lewis said later, "I could not know at the time that I was looking at the person whom the Lord had chosen to translate the Book of Mormon, the Doctrine and Covenants, and the Pearl of Great Price. I thought I was there to buy real estate."

Sister Vy was taught the gospel in her home by Brother Lewis and Captain William Shumate, a returned missionary then stationed in Saigon. She alone from all her family was baptized into the Church. The ordinance took place at the Saigon Branch building. Her first calling was to translate a Church pamphlet titled "Joseph Smith's Testimony" for the second time. Some Vietnamese members and investigators were having difficulty understanding a prior translation that was based on a word-for-word approach. She took the pamphlet home and read it over and over throughout the night. Then she began to write. A strange feeling came over her as if an unseen hand was helping her. She could feel the meaning of the words in her heart and mind and translated according to the feelings and impressions she had. The Spirit filled her soul with light and power. As she translated under the influence of the Spirit, she gained a sure testimony that Joseph Smith was a prophet and that the Book of Mormon, which she had not yet read, was true. She knew she had been helped in an unusual manner by an unseen power, but she did not recognize at the time that the Holy Spirit directed her in the translation and bore witness of the truth. What is said of the Lord's hand in finding Sister Vy is true for all three of us: Cao Minh, Sister Vy, and myself. From all the millions of Vietnamese, His hand plucked us from the masses and placed us in a position to hear the gospel and do His work. We three and also others the Lord selected would yet be involved in translating many important things by the Spirit, including the Book of Mormon.

When I was baptized, the leadership of the branch and most of the members were American military or civilians working for the U.S. government or private businesses. The majority of the LDS military in Saigon attended the servicemen's group at Tan Son Nhut military base. Soon after my baptism, I was called as an interpreter to help the Mormon servicemen who attended the Saigon Branch to teach the gospel to my Vietnamese brothers and sisters. These faithful men took upon themselves President David O. McKay's "every member a missionary" challenge. This occurred not only in Saigon but also wherever faithful LDS soldiers, sailors, airmen, or marines were based in my country. They reached out to their brothers in arms first and then to their Vietnamese associates.

There was consistently a 1 percent LDS ratio in the American military serving in Vietnam, peaking at about 5,500 LDS in 1968. The LDS Church in the Republic of Vietnam was organized into three districts: the Northern, Central, and Southern Districts. The Saigon Branch and the nearby Tan Son Nhut and Bien Hoa Groups were part of the Southern District. It is these three with which I am most familiar.

On October 10, 1966, just a month after my baptism, another important event took place. Along with the date of my baptism, I consider this event to be the beginning of my new life. On that day, from the top floor of the Caravelle Hotel in downtown Saigon, Elder Gordon B. Hinckley dedicated the land of Vietnam for the preaching of the gospel. My call as an interpreter coincided with the dedication of my country for missionary work. I felt that the Lord's hand was in these events. I felt a great weight to accurately convey the gospel to the Vietnamese in our native tongue.

The dedication came about in an interesting way. Elder Hinckley and Elder Marion D. Hanks came to visit various servicemen's groups in Vietnam and to give counsel and comfort to members of the Church. One of their meetings was held in the rooftop garden room of the Caravelle Hotel. Over two hundred LDS civilians and servicemen and servicewomen were in attendance. Elder Hanks spoke about the two battles the servicemen were fighting; only one was with the invading army from the North. The other, more important battle was the battle every person must fight, the battle against Satan to return to our Heavenly Father. He counseled them to remain true and faithful to their covenants and to return home with honor. Elder Hinckley then spoke at length and gave further valuable counsel. When Elder Hinckley finished his remarks, he paused for a long moment, causing everyone to wonder why he had stopped speaking. The question was answered when Elder Hinckley informed the congregation that President David O. McKay had authorized him to dedicate the land of Vietnam for missionary work if he felt led by the Spirit to do so. Much to the surprise and delight of those present, he indicated he wanted to do so at that time.

In dedicating and setting apart the land, Elder Hinckley offered a beautiful prayer, which included this observation and request: "We have seen in other parts of Asia the manner in which Thou hast turned the hand and the work of the adversary to the good and the blessing of many of Thy children. And now we call upon Thee at this time that Thou wilt similarly pour out Thy Spirit upon this land." He also asked the Lord "to open the way for the coming of the missionaries and make their labors fruitful of great and everlasting good in the lives of the people." He asked that the Lord's Spirit be poured out upon nonmembers that they would be more willing to hear the gospel of Jesus Christ and upon those who already had the gospel so that they would be more willing to share it. (See *Church News,* November 19, 1966; R. Lanier Britsch, *From the East* [Salt Lake City: Deseret Book, 1998]; *Improvement Era,* June 1968, 48–50.)

This prayer was answered in direct ways in my life. I listened to Airman Moore and I accepted the gospel; now I was willing to share the gospel with others. One of those others was my future wife, Le My Lien. When I was baptized, Lien (pronounced LEEN) was among the first investigators I was asked to assist in my calling as interpreter for the branch missionaries. She and four of her sisters wanted to learn about the gospel. They lived with their mother, Mai, and two younger brothers and one more little sister, none of whom investigated the gospel at that time. Mother Mai, whose husband had recently died, reluctantly permitted the five sisters to investigate the new religion. Lien was the third sister. Because the missionary tracts were predominantly in English, I was asked to accompany the branch missionaries and help translate the Church literature for Lien and her sisters. In so doing, my own gospel knowledge increased. Lien and I thus learned many gospel concepts together as she received the discussions and I translated.

It was also my privilege to occasionally accompany the three older sisters and their aunt, all younger than I, to social activities, such as going to a restaurant or to a movie. This happy (for me) group fellowshipping—four beautiful young ladies with a single young man—did not go unnoticed by other young men. What, they wondered, was Tay's secret with the ladies? Sometimes they would observe this scrawny young man with such an attractive group of ladies and need to satisfy their curiosity.

"Why," they would ask, "are you in the company of so many young women?"

"I am trying to select a wife from among these sisters," I said. The sisters would play along.

"Which one will you choose?" they inquired with obvious envy.

"I do not know," I said in a weary tone. "I must continue my research."

In truth, I had already made my selection in my heart, although no one knew but me. Any one of the sisters would be a good wife, but I followed the call of my heart and chose the one I felt was most choice in spirit. In my eyes, Lien was also the most beautiful. In my association with Lien, I learned that she had special qualities of humility and propriety and was a virtuous young woman in whose presence I felt happy. I drank into my private thoughts her goodness and beauty and found myself continually thirsty for more. I began to hope the Church would send more pamphlets so I could see her even more often in the future. In the propriety of our chaperoned meetings to discuss the gospel and also in our group activities, I began to look upon her as a potential mate. When we learned about temple marriage, I pictured her as the one across the altar. When we talked about the importance of families in the Church, I pictured a family of Lien and me and our as yet unborn children. I felt new tingling sensations in my heart when I was with her and emptiness when we were apart. I was too shy to inquire if she felt as I did. We did not go out alone—only as a group. I was falling in love, but how was she to know? I kept my feelings in my heart. I felt I had too little to offer.

Meanwhile, the missionaries' efforts bore fruit. Lien's two oldest sisters were baptized into the Church after about two months of missionary discussions. A few months later, the two younger sisters accepted the gospel and were baptized. Lien was not yet ready. Inasmuch as Lien became my wife long before she was baptized, I can safely say that with her my teaching efforts, which worked well with her sisters, were impaired by her distracting charm and beauty.

These were happy times for me. My first taste of missionary work and the value of translating gospel ideas into my native language made a joyful impression on my soul. The branch members opened their hearts and homes to me. I had more friends than ever before in my life. Dinners and social gatherings and gospel discussions buoyed my spirits and stimulated my mind. I loved my new associations in the branch as my circle of friends increased not only in number but also in quality.

My childhood fears of being alone and forever sad in this world faded in the glow of each Sunday morning and each newfound friend in the gospel. I enjoyed my translation work in my Church calling and felt satisfaction in my contribution to missionary work. I received training frequently in more advanced English at USAID and thereby improved my language skills. My financial needs were met, and I was able to help my sister and, through my tithing and fast offerings, help others as well. I was very happy with my new life.

I was also grateful that, so far, I had not been directly involved with the war. Realistically, I knew that my good fortune could not last. As the communists advanced on the South, it was weighing upon my conscience to work peacefully for the Americans and serve my church as a translator while my country was being overrun. I felt uncomfortable, if not worthless, standing beside my uniformed branch members, both Vietnamese and American, who were engaged in the battle to save my country while I did nothing. My sense of duty often did battle with my common sense. In any case, whether or not I served in the army was out of my hands. Poor health had deferred me from the draft for four years, but now my country's need for manpower was increasing, and old deferments were no longer valid. It was my duty to serve if called. Our liberties were at stake, and the tide was turning against us. I did not want to kill my brothers from the North, but I also did not want to sit by and see my country be absorbed into a communist regime. I was being carried toward the war like a piece of driftwood on a fast-moving river. Its current was pulling me closer and closer to the falls. I was powerless to avoid the war awaiting me downstream. There was no escape. It was only a matter of time until the current drew me over the falls and into the vortex.

CHAPTER 4

In Defense of Liberty

When I was twenty-five years old, in the summer of 1968, the Army of the Republic of Vietnam (ARVN) drafted me into military service. Even though I knew such a notice was coming, I was no less devastated when it happened. It was less than two years since my baptism. It seemed that I had no sooner found fellowship among the Latter-day Saints and had the light of the gospel glowing within me than I was plucked from my Saigon haven.

The Saigon Saints shared in my sadness at my separation from their fellowship. Cao Minh, Sister Vy, and others embraced me and wished me well. Some of the men in the Saigon Branch were already in the military and were familiar with its ways. I received warnings and much counsel and guidance from these friends as to how to conduct myself in the jungle of war. Their stories of death brought to mind the smell of corpses when I was seven. It was a revolting memory. No one wanted to avoid death more than I did, so I eagerly soaked up any information they offered to help me preserve my life: how to detect booby traps, how to prevent infections in my feet and to keep them dry, how to recognize an ambush, and how to endure the rain day after day without shelter. I don't know if I felt better or worse after such an education.

My heart ached to stay within my gospel associations, but it was not to be. One day I wore a suit and carried the scriptures as a translator at missionary discussions about the gospel of peace; the next day I wore an army uniform and carried an M-16 rifle and was being instructed about how to best kill the enemy. The contrast could not have been greater and was only exceeded by the contrast of my former happiness with my dreaded future. Worst of all was the indefinite length of service I faced. Although my activation in the army officer reserves was officially for four years, there was a big *if* involved. It was well known that a draftee into the army, North or South, was expected to fight on until victory or death. (As to the latter option, in the course of the war approximately 254,300 soldiers from the South and 1,027,000 from the North were released from their service by dying in combat. By comparison, 408,000 Americans died in World War II. Of the more than 1.5 million Americans stationed inside Vietnam between 1965 and 1973, some 58,000 died in the Vietnam War.)

If a draftee was lucky, perhaps some nonfatal but debilitating wound would save him from further combat. In my case, I knew that *if* the war were won, the four-year timeline would be honored; otherwise, I was there to stay. Nothing about the army fit into the plans I had made for the rest of my life. I wanted to marry Lien and help spread the gospel in Vietnam. Someday, I wanted to go to the house of the Lord and participate in the sealing ordinances for myself and my departed loved ones. I had that "woe is me" feeling of my childhood all over again.

My personal problems and trepidations were insignificant and, in fact, invisible in the vast scheme of things in the year of 1968. War protests in America were growing and spreading across the country. Mounting U.S. casualties were fueled by the willingness of the North to take massive casualties of their own in exchange for demoralizing coverage of American deaths on the evening news.

The most important event of the war came to be known as the Tet Offensive. It was the reason my deferment was cancelled and I was drafted. It was the reason the United States withdrew their forces from Vietnam. It was the reason Saigon eventually fell and its Saints were scattered. This military offensive, the turning point of the war, occurred on January 30 and 31, 1968, at the time of the Vietnamese Lunar New Year, or Tet. For several thousand years, Tet had been a time of celebration and peace in Vietnam. North Vietnam agreed to the usual truce during the days of this important holiday, which is also observed throughout Asia. Both Vietnamese armies and all the villages in Vietnam celebrated as usual, except the North celebrated a day early. When the South celebrated, they let their guard down. The Tet Offensive simultaneously unleashed blood and gore from one end of my country to the other. The North Vietnamese killed 119 Americans and 363 South Vietnamese soldiers at the cost of over 8,000 deaths among their own forces. An additional 5,400 South Vietnamese civilians were killed in the attacks. All of these deaths occurred during Tet's scheduled "truce."

Even with America's decisive military victory during Tet, the reaction in the United States was one of total shock over their own losses. Observing this reaction, the communists made the death of any American by any means their primary goal, because without American help, the South was a much weaker foe. The strategy worked. In response to the Tet Offensive and the war protests it spawned, President Johnson declined to run for reelection, and all competing candidates pledged to withdraw U.S. forces.

Meanwhile, in my country, the North Vietnamese seemed to be everywhere except in Saigon. In the villages and towns outside of Saigon, mortar attacks, elusive snipers, and violent acts such as summary execution, rape, throat slashing, and the torching of villages were rampant. The North recruited many villagers as allies by threatening their lives if they did not cooperate in the "liberation." The South Vietnamese Army threatened these same villagers if they did not cooperate in repelling the aggression from the North. If villagers were suspected of being sympathetic to the North, their crops were frequently shot up, trampled, or burned. To preserve their crops, not to mention their lives, many chose to be friendly with the South Vietnamese Army by day and friendly with the North Vietnamese forces by night.

With these historical events and conditions swirling in my mind, I reported to Thu Duc Officer Training School for nine months of training. Although I was in frail health and did not appear to have merit as a soldier, I nevertheless began my training as an officer trainee. What a sight I must have been! I was so small! Goliath probably didn't laugh at David as much as some people laughed at me. I was trained to use three rifles: the M-1, the carbine, and the M-16. The biggest was the M-1 rifle. It was quite heavy for me to carry, and when I stood it on end by my side, it was taller than I was. If I attached a bayonet, it towered over me. When I fired a round, the rifle discharge produced a recoil kick that jammed the butt of the rifle into my shoulder with sufficient force to nearly knock me down. If I was already down, as in the prone position on the firing range, the kick produced huge, deep bruises on my shoulder. I have heard Americans speak of the "ninety-seven pound weakling" who is so pathetic he is encouraged to lift weights to build up his body. "Ninety-seven pound weakling," you say? "Pathetic," you say? I was twenty-two pounds short of qualifying for such a title! At seventy-five pounds, I even fell short of my army's own regulations. They had a requirement that stated a soldier must weigh a minimum of thirty-five kilograms (seventy-seven pounds) to qualify for military service in general and for combat in particular. The rigors of carrying full combat gear into battle were not deemed feasible for men weighing less than the requirement. Unfeasible or not, I found myself in combat soon enough. My only consolation was that I made a very small target.

I prayed to God that I could be as Samuel the Lamanite, who stood upon the city wall and preached God's word. When his enemies tried to sling their arrows and kill him, no matter how well they aimed, no matter how many times they tried, they could not hit Samuel. I prayed for the same results for those who shot at me. I was afraid. I prayed continually in my heart for my protection.

I prayed for the safety of Lien. I prayed she would accept baptism. She said she was not yet fully converted. I was patient. Changing religions is no small matter. Only the Holy Ghost can convince one of the truth by bearing witness to one's spirit. Lien's reluctance was not entirely due to new concepts that were difficult to fully understand. Lien's mother reacted to Lien's sisters' conversions somewhat as Ba had toward my baptism. She was puzzled and disappointed. Lien was reluctant to add to her mother's sadness by joining her sisters in the waters of baptism. I prayed that her mother's heart would be softened. I wrote letters to Lien and made my feelings known.

Occasionally, during training, I was granted a weekend leave and could actually see Lien. I took her on our first date without her sisters. She seemed even more beautiful and more choice than when I last saw her. I think the same young men who had envied my "group date" with Lien and all her sisters would still ask if they saw me with only Lien, "What is Tay's secret?"

I also took great pleasure in seeing my friends at the Saigon Branch. In those days, if I went away for a month or two, there were a few new converts and a few newly assigned American replacements to meet upon my return. Going home was very frustrating, because I knew I had to go back to my unit. Worse yet, after nine months, when officers' school was over, I would face my first encounters with combat.

I successfully completed my officer training and was promoted to warrant officer, an entry-level officer rank. My first assignment after officers' school was near Bien Hoa Air Base, about twenty miles from Saigon. As a warrant officer, I commanded a platoon, which placed me over about forty-five men. A platoon had three squads of fifteen men each. My platoon was assigned to the Bien Hoa Province Regional Defense Militia to protect a small area, including around the air base, from North Vietnamese attacks. We were part of a mobile company and moved frequently, one week here and another week there. We slept in the jungles on the ground, in the rain, in the mud, in the heat, and in the swarms of insects. The most humble home of my childhood was a palace compared to life in the field. My old plank bed seemed luxurious in my memory. Between operations in the field, we stayed in the villages among the people. We slept in schools or other public buildings. Mainly, week in and week out, our provincial militia searched for North Vietnamese forces and expelled them by force from the province of Bien Hoa. The neighboring province thus inherited the unwelcome invaders from the North and tried to return our favor by expelling those forces from their province back into ours. Only the dead were permitted to drop out of this deadly game. This cat-and-mouse drama was not conducive to ending hostilities; it only relocated them. This made us feel that our efforts were of no real value. We relied on our government leaders and the American leaders to negotiate a just peace. Until that happened, we sought to retain our own lives. I always did my duty, but I was no hero, nor did I seek to be one.

At all times, the Lord answered my prayers to guide my assignments. This assignment was bad, yes, but it could have been much worse. In the Regional Defense Militia, I was not subject to being transferred. It was certainly a better duty than being assigned to the regular army. In the regular army, soldiers went from battlefront to battlefront, always where there was heavy combat. These areas had high concentrations of troops accompanied by heavy artillery and tanks. There were many opportunities to die. Around Bien Hoa, enemy soldiers were more spread out and not so heavily armed. Death was not a stranger, but it was not as common as on the battlefront. In Bien Hoa, the enemy moved around the jungle, hiding in trees or tunnels in the ground by day and attacking by night. They sought to ambush and kill patrols such as mine. We sought to find them before they found us.

When you are fighting, the war is not the big war going on all over the country; it is the war within you and the war immediately around you. It is behind every tree, around every bend of the river, across every rice paddy. It is remembering what has happened before and anticipating what might happen next. It is in the shadows. It is in your mind. It is in every waking moment, for you never know when an enemy will strike or from where. It is in every sleeping moment when you place your life in the hands of your sentry and hope he gives you sufficient warning if an attack comes. If he fails in his duty and falls asleep, you might be killed in your sleep. The war fills your thoughts by day and your dreams by night. It is your cold food, your wet feet, and your insect-infested bed. The war takes over your life and tempts you with death as a means of relief. Some men die instantly as artillery or grenades blow them apart. Others die painfully slow deaths, infected with booby-trap wounds, disease, or mental torment. Others harden into nonhumans and live to fight another day. Many men become animals. They forsake good and embrace evil. They heed the adversary's call to "eat, drink, and be merry for tomorrow we die." For some, tomorrow, if not sooner, they do die. Some of these men were under my command. The men I wished to be with were the faithful brethren of the Saigon Branch, where God's name was held in reverence and the Spirit was comfortable within its walls. The branch was a piece of heaven. It provided an oasis of love and fellowship among the Saints. Within its walls, the war seemed distant and powerless. The songs of Zion brought peace to my heart. The sacrament turned my thoughts to my Redeemer. The testimonies and the lessons increased my confidence and interest in the future. The war, in stark contrast, was nothing short of hell. I continually prayed for a way out.

I also prayed about Lien and my desire for a future together. Although I had little to offer and life was uncertain, my love for Lien had grown to the point where I felt compelled to seek her hand in marriage. She had not yet fully accepted the gospel, but I knew she was a choice woman and the one I wanted to marry. It was selfish to ask her to marry me when my life was in such danger, but her love was such that she accepted my proposal. We decided to take our chances and be together as long as we could. We were married during one of my infrequent trips to Saigon, at Brother Robert S. Lewis's home. He was branch president at the time, and the branch held meetings in his home, located on the main road between downtown Saigon and the Saigon Airport. He had a large living room that served as a dance floor for our wedding reception. A live band played as all the branch members congratulated Lien and me and gave us presents and good wishes for our future together.

Two days after our marriage, I returned to my combat unit. Meanwhile, Lien, an excellent typist, was hired by the branch translation committee to type the committee's completed pamphlets into Vietnamese. I felt this was a blessing because she was exposed to the gospel teachings on a regular basis. Once back in combat, with my new responsibilities as a husband, I was more concerned than ever about my situation. I had a keen desire to escape the horrors of combat and to return to my home.

On one occasion especially, my faith was tried. I was reassigned to the ARVN Eighteenth Division, the regular army. This felt like a death sentence to me. I recoiled from the very thought of increased opportunities for combat. Most of the South Vietnamese ARVN casualties of war in those days were from the ranks of regular army forces in units such as the one to which I had been reassigned. I was very worried about my future. In my mind, I could see myself lying dead, facedown in the muddy field of some village, other soldiers stepping over me, with no concern or regard for Tay. I could picture my dear Lien struggling with no Tay to help. I tried to block out such thoughts. Perhaps the Lord had heard me complain too often about my trials, and He had grown weary of the murmuring in my heart. Perhaps He would show me how bad my assignment could be. I knew that all I had been through would seem like child's play compared to frontline duty. I prayed mightily for the Lord to reverse this dangerous situation.

I reported as ordered to my new commander in the regular army. He looked pitifully at me and looked in my personnel file. Remember that weight regulation? The commander glanced through my thick file. His eyes suddenly stopped where it said, "Tay is unsuitable for combat duty." I think God led his eyes to those words and also enflamed his ego. The commander suddenly became very angry, not with me, but with those who had transferred me into his command. "I will not accept a replacement officer unfit for combat," he declared with great indignity. Two days later, I was back in my old unit. Suddenly, I was happy to be there. God does work in mysterious ways.

Happiness, however, wears off quickly in the jungle. Even though we saw the enemy face-to-face only about once every week or two on average, we knew they were there. We could hear their incoming mortar shells whistling through the air. We could hear their bullets zip by our heads and snap twigs in the trees we took cover behind. We saw their camps and avoided their booby traps. We could smell their dead from a kilometer away. I could smell *them* from two kilometers away.

Always we sought out the North Vietnamese, and always they hid from us until they could devise an ambush or a hit-and-run strike. Just knowing they were always around and then suffering the effects of their presence when they finally showed themselves was sufficient to keep our nerves frayed and our lives miserable.

The Lord watched over me well during my combat experiences. I was sick for weeks at a time because of overexposure to the extreme tropical heat alternated with heavy downpours of drenching rain, but I was never wounded or seriously injured. My prayers to be like Samuel the Lamanite were answered where the enemy's aim was concerned. When bullets started to fly, however, I was not bold like Samuel, standing defiantly on the wall. I was more like a quivering little rabbit, hunched down on the ground, doing my duty to shoot back, but also doing my part to avoid their bullets.

Often when we were sent in search of the enemy, we were met by ambushes or mine traps. Some of my comrades lost their lives as they fought beside me. On one occasion, I walked as the second man in a single-file line through the jungle. The soldier behind me tripped a hidden line connected to a claymore mine. It exploded and killed him. The dead man lost his legs and his torso split open, adding his blood to the blood-soaked ground of my country. The blast also injured the man in front of me and the fourth man in line. Through God's grace, I was not injured.

On another occasion, a North Vietnamese soldier watched our platoon from a distance. We moved in single file about fifteen feet apart. As we approached a place where a string of mines was laid to match our spacing, he pulled a long line from his remote position that was supposed to cause a chain reaction of explosions to kill us all. Instead, the first explosion, rigged in an old artillery shell aimed at the line of mines, blew out the back end of the shell casing. This caused the force of the blast to disperse without focus. The concussion from the blast, or maybe God's fist, broke the next mine in line in two pieces, and it failed to explode. This nipped in the bud the planned chain reaction of mine explosions. Otherwise, I would surely have died, ensnared in this well-laid trap like a fish in a net. Without God's kind mercies, there was no possible escape; we all could have died.

On these and many other occasions, I can gratefully testify that Heavenly Father always protected me and preserved my life in spite of the many dangers I was called to face in my army assignments. After one year in combat He also helped with a timely promotion and transfer that prevented me from dying of exposure to the elements. At that time, I was promoted to second lieutenant and reassigned to be co-commander of a company of 135 men. This was beneficial for two reasons. First, the commander or his co-commander made assignments as to which platoons went into the field but rarely had to go themselves. Second, my commander liked me. He was a first lieutenant. Company commanders are normally captains or majors, but our officer ranks were very thin, so lower-ranking officers assumed increased responsibilities. My commander was a kind and civil man. He took an interest in my life. He made it possible for me to go to Saigon to see my wife much more frequently than my previous assignment allowed. I had usually been within twenty to forty miles of my home, but it may as well have been four hundred miles for the good it did. It was illegal to leave one's post unless on official leave or on army business. Such opportunities were rare in the past. Now my new commander permitted me to do army business in Saigon two or three times per month. It was a prayer fulfilled every time I saw my beloved Lien. On one happy occasion I learned she was pregnant. I was thrilled. And I was worried.

Whenever I was home on Sunday, I would attend the Saigon Branch and partake of the Lord's supper and sing the songs of Zion. I often sang my favorite hymns to myself while on duty in the field. Except for my visits to the Saigon Branch, I attended no church. I made up my own sermons in my mind. Saying the words of the hymns was like hearing a sermon. I could not sing hymns out loud, but I could quietly hum them or think about the words in my mind. "Did You Think to Pray?" "Love at Home." "I Need Thee Every Hour." "How Great the Wisdom and the Love." All were comforting in the absence of those I loved. How I missed Lien! How I missed Cao Minh and Sister Vy! The "old-timers" were ever faithful, and the little branch was growing steadily. There were only a dozen or so Vietnamese Saints when I joined the Church, and now there were over fifty. Sister Vy made steady progress in translating the Book of Mormon, and Brother Cao Minh assisted her in editing. My wife was hired at the time the committee was provided a typewriter. She assisted Sister Vy and Cao Minh by typing the finished handwritten pages in Vietnamese. When I came to church, some recent converts and newly assigned Americans thought I was a new member in the Saigon Branch. I was a stranger to them, but I soon got acquainted and rejoiced in new friendships. I needed all the fellowship I could get from the members of the branch and my family. My gospel associations gave me hope for a better day to come when peace and safety would prevail.

So far the Lord had protected me. Still, I could not expect such favored treatment to last forever. I could not forget that in a combat unit such as mine there was no time limit placed on my services. I always remembered the terms: fight until you win or until you die. Even my less hazardous duties as company co-commander were still hazardous; I was a small but prized target for the enemy. I was still being shot at, although not as frequently as before. It stood to reason that if I served in a combat unit year after year, I would eventually be killed or wounded. With no end to the hostilities in sight, it was unlikely that I would be spared the fate of so many of my comrades. With Lien pregnant, the likelihood of my becoming a casualty caused me increased anxiety. I began to worry that I would never see my baby. I began to picture another little boy without a father. I recalled all my days of loneliness and misery when I was a little boy and had no parents. I began to pray mightily for the Lord to save me. I prayed as never before. I prayed as Enos, all day and all night. I could see no way out of my perilous circumstances, but I trusted that God could find a way for me. Once again, God heard and answered my prayers.

A few months later, God opened a door for me to leave my combat assignment behind me. After more than two years of combat duty, I learned from an army circular that language teachers were needed in the Armed Forces Language School in Saigon. My heart rate doubled when I contemplated the possibilities. I worried about my skill level, because I had had few opportunities to speak English in the army. Sometimes, we did joint operations with the Americans or the Australians, and I served as interpreter. Still, I doubted my proficiency and recognized my limited talents. I prayed for God's help so I could remember all that I had been taught in my high school studies and at USAID. Excited and hopeful beyond my capacity to endure for very long, I immediately applied to teach English and took the necessary examinations. Oh, how I prayed that the Lord would assist me in being reassigned to teach English at that school! My hopes were raised so high by the opening of this door, I knew I would be crushed beyond recovery if it were slammed in my face. I had one foot in the door, but there was opposition to my passing through it. Some of my leaders seemed happy for my new opportunity; others seemed jealous. One high commander asked, "Why should Tay leave the fighting and I stay?" There seemed to be a tug-of-war going on behind the scenes over which I had no control. I prayed continually and thanked God for the door He had opened and pleaded with Him to let me enter. After some weeks of nerve-wracking suspense, I received my new orders. I praised God! I was ecstatic! I was accepted as a teacher at the language school and was permanently reassigned to Saigon. In the same month, my first child, our son Vu, was born. I thanked my Heavenly Father for blessing me that my son would have a father and that I would have a son!

Mere words cannot express the terrible conditions and happenings of war, nor can they express my extreme happiness when I was reassigned to a noncombat position that allowed me to be with my family again. It was a miracle to me. My life was transformed back to the peace and brotherhood among the Saints that I had cherished and dreamed of when walking terrified through the jungles and fields of Bien Hoa Province.

Because of my new assignment in Saigon, I was able to attend church services regularly at the Saigon Branch. I was soon called as a counselor in the branch presidency. Brother Ralph Kurihara was then serving as branch president. (He replaced my friend Cao Minh, who had previously replaced Brother Lewis and served until his military assignment took him away from the Saigon area.) At that time, in the summer of 1971, native Vietnamese members numbered about eighty, and the Church was just beginning to grow in Vietnam. My new assignment with the army gave me Sundays off and allowed me to mingle again with the Saigon Saints. I renewed old friendships and nurtured new ones. As a member of the branch presidency, I met some of the members by appointment to issue callings or to counsel with them about some problem or other. I was always involved to some degree with branch activities and socials. In this way, I became better acquainted with the members and also with the way a branch of the Church functions.

Sister Vy still lived in the country, where she did most of her translation work, but still came to church regularly on Sundays and continued to serve as Relief Society president. We became even better friends and enjoyed conversing with one another in three languages: French, English, and Vietnamese.

Le Van Kha, newly baptized in 1971, soon became my close friend. He was very faithful with a strong testimony of the gospel, but his family, already members of another Christian sect, did not follow his lead. They maintained that they were already baptized and that repeating the ordinance was unnecessary. Still, they attended branch meetings and participated in the activities.

In November 1971, while continuing to serve in the branch presidency, I was called to be on the translation committee. I joined Sister Vy and Cao Minh and others in the work of translating scriptures and Church teaching materials. The translation committee, with Sister Vy as head translator and President Bradshaw as chairman, operated under the direction of the Church's Translation Services Department in Salt Lake City. Although translation work in Vietnam had begun as early as 1963, the committee was not officially organized until 1969. In that year, after an extensive tour of Asia, Elder Ezra Taft Benson recommended that the Book of Mormon and other Church materials be translated and made available in three additional languages. They were Thai, Indonesian, and Vietnamese. The presiding Brethren approved Elder Benson's proposal, and translation committees were quickly established in each country to do the work. The Translation Services Department's area manager was Brother Kan Watanabe in Tokyo, who oversaw work in five Asian languages. The translation committee in the Saigon Branch sent monthly reports to Brother Watanabe about the work being done. Locally, the committee's work was supervised by the Vietnam Southern District president and the Hong Kong mission president. I was happy to be available to serve in such a worthy cause as translating Church material for the Vietnamese Saints and investigators. (Details in this paragraph were verified in John E. Carr's history of the Church Translation Department, *For in That Day: A History of Translation and Distribution, 1965–1980* [Utah: n.p., 1980].)

It was just plain wonderful to be in the fellowship of the Saints again. To be with men of culture and women of virtue was refreshment to my soul. After two years of combat duty, I respected good people and appreciated good friends more deeply than ever before. The growing branch moved to a larger rented facility. It was located in the Vietnamese American Association School located in Saigon. Even as we outgrew our facilities and found a better place to meet, we were clearly aware of the things we didn't have. We knew we had a long way to go. From our Mormon military friends, we heard about wonderful meeting facilities, such as the Tabernacle on Temple Square. It was hard to imagine so many Saints under one roof. It was a sight I longed to see. Some described their stake centers and wards back home.

We were only a small branch, but we Saigon Saints wanted to be full participants in the gospel of Jesus Christ. We shared a dream of someday having our own chapel, our own stake center, and finally our own temple in Vietnam. The Church was growing in Asia. Japan had many thousands of members, the first seeds of whom sprouted from the ashes of World War II. Some of us were aware of the Church's presence in another divided country, Korea. Beginning with the missionary efforts of LDS servicemen stationed in South Korea, the seeds of the gospel were planted there. After the Korean War, full-time missionaries were sent, and many thousands of South Koreans joined the Church. Already, in less than twenty years, they had many wards and some stakes. We thought the work in Vietnam would take a similar course. This is the very thing Elder Gordon B. Hinckley prayed for that day atop the Caravelle Hotel when he dedicated Vietnam for the preaching of the gospel. South Korea was blessed to attain a stable peace and a secure border with North Korea. This enabled South Korea to develop as a free nation in which their country and the gospel flourished. To repeat this pattern in South Vietnam was our fond desire. We could feel the Lord's Spirit and see the potential of our people. This motivated us to think positively about the future and to seek out others to teach. The work of translating gospel ideals into Vietnamese was one of the keys to expanding the work. It also fulfilled the Lord's directive to teach all people in their native tongue. In moments of inadequacy, I wished I had better language skills and was closer to the Spirit so that I might make a more worthy contribution to the work of translating. I knew I needed to improve myself in both areas. The Lord must have agreed, because He provided me with an unexpected opportunity.

CHAPTER 5

The Distant Shores of Freedom

My path to improvement was revealed to me in the spring of 1972. Twenty-five Vietnamese linguists stationed at the Armed Forces Language School in Saigon were selected to go to the United States for six months of advanced language training at Lackland Air Force Base in San Antonio, Texas. I was one of those selected. It thrilled me to know I would soon visit the United States of America. Such training would also help me in my translation assignments within the branch. The thought of being separated from Lien, who was pregnant, and my little son, Vu, provided my only sad contemplation. Still, I considered it a wonderful opportunity to increase my language skills and see for myself the great bastion of power, freedom, and prosperity that was America. To visit the distant shores of freedom I had heard and read so much about, the country to which we owed our present liberty, for me outweighed the inconvenience of a long separation from Lien and Vu. They were in good hands among the members of the Saigon Branch, and I trusted that I was partly on an errand for the Lord and that God would watch over them in my absence.

Before my departure, President William S. Bradshaw, president of the Hong Kong Mission, came to Saigon to attend a Southern District conference. Two servicemen's groups—the Bien Hoa Group, and the Tan Son Nhut Group—as well as the Saigon Branch were all in the Southern District. When President Bradshaw was informed of my upcoming trip to the United States, he took me aside and told me he wished to provide me with a temple recommend. I did not think of this myself. I should have. Would that not bring me closer to the Spirit, and was that not what I prayed for? Yes. Still, I hesitated to act. There was no temple in Texas, and I had no idea what my travel opportunities would be in America. President Bradshaw was firm. He advised me to take a temple recommend with me and said that the Lord might provide a way for me to go to the Salt Lake Temple. President Bradshaw interviewed me and issued my recommend. I found that having a recommend was a blessing in itself, whether I went to the temple or not. Simply being found worthy to attend the temple and to have that little paper to remind me of my standing with the Lord was in itself humbling and inspiring. I felt closer to the Spirit already. I tucked the recommend away and prayed I would be able to use it.

With twenty-four of my Vietnamese comrades, I traveled to America to attend the six-month course in English-teaching skills at the Defense Language Institute at Lackland Air Force Base. My initial views of America were from airports and military bases, but gradually, as time permitted and restrictions eased, I was able to see a slice of America.

I was amazed with the American highway system, the automobiles, the homes, the supermarkets, and the vastness of the land itself. That the land mass of one American state, Texas, was as large as Vietnam, Cambodia, Laos, and most of Thailand

SOUTHERN DISTRICT CONFERENCE,
TAN SON NHUT AIR BASE CHAPEL, DECEMBER, 1971
SPEAKER AT PULPIT: Virgil N. Kovalenko, Bien Hoa group leader
THIRD FROM PULPIT: Nguyen Cao Minh
RIGHT: President William S. Bradshaw

(photograph courtesy John D. Parr)

was remarkable to me, as was the expanse of open, undeveloped, and unpopulated land. There is plenty of room here for Tay, I thought to myself.

The wealth of the average American compared to the average Vietnamese was staggering. Most people seemed to have everything they needed and much more, far beyond their needs. In a way, I had believed that Saigon was somewhat "Americanized" because of the American military influence. But when I saw everyday American civilians going about their business without worry or strife, and when I saw modern skyscrapers, shopping malls, telephones that always worked, televisions with twenty channels, and supermarkets with ten different brands of string beans, I knew I had been naive. I had realized that the vegetable stall Ba and I ran in the marketplace at Phu Nhuan could not compare to the produce department at a Safeway store, but I had thought perhaps the Americanized food or entertainment or fashions in Saigon might be found in America. Nothing was comparable. Parts of Saigon were merely vulgar, counterfeit versions of America. They catered to the needs of men whose lives were reduced by the war to the lowest levels of moral behavior. In America, the people I met were completely different from the average American in Viet-nam. They were good and decent, and they were unarmed. I believe the best things about America will always be in America. The Book of Mormon declaration that this land, because of its inspired Constitution, is a land of promise, a land choice above all other lands, a land destined to prosper if righteous, was made clear to me. Abundantly clear.

The Armed Forces Language School was comprehensive and very helpful to me but not very demanding. We had classes six or seven hours a day during the week and had weekends off. This was more free time than my friends and I were used to. Many of my fellow students, all with families or loved ones in Vietnam, took the opportunity to turn spare time into extra income. There were homes being built in the area and civilian contractors right on the base. Some of the Vietnamese students were skilled at painting or had other construction-related talents. Some were merely willing to do anything to earn some extra money for themselves and their families back home. After classes and on weekends, most of my group worked at one of the construction sites near the base. The U.S. Air Force granted access, if not permission, to and from the base, so it seemed silly not to work. The work could be justified as exposure to practical English, even though many of the workers spoke no English. The Vietnamese students thus had an advantage over many visiting Mexican workers competing for the same jobs. The wages were shrugged at locally, but for low-ranking Vietnamese army officers they beckoned like the compensation of generals.

As for myself, I had brought my own work with me. I translated Church brochures such as "After Baptism, What?" and others so that when I returned, they could be used to teach the new Vietnamese Saints and investigators. Still, I was not oblivious to the opportunity to benefit from America's wealth. The United States provided our housing and gave us six dollars per day to pay for food. I always limited myself to one dollar or less, thereby saving five dollars per day to take home with me. That alone would be considered a good wage by most workers in Vietnam. Many times, for thirty-seven cents, I bought a small, cooked chicken at the base commissary. I usually ate only once per day. My language school roommate had similar goals to save money. Sometimes, we bought food together and prepared it in our room to stay under our one-dollar budget.

Early on during my time at Lackland Air Force Base, I found the LDS branch of the Church and attended meetings. Mormons stationed there met on the base in a chapel shared with other faiths. An LDS chaplain oversaw the use of the chapel when the Latter-day Saints met. This reminded me of my early experience in Vietnam, when most of the members and leadership were LDS servicemen. At one such meeting, I met two LDS servicemen stationed at Lackland who normally attended church off base with their girlfriends in a regular ward. For some reason, on that day they attended the same meeting I did. They introduced themselves, and we talked at length. I explained my Church background and my presence on the base. They invited me to attend the off-base ward the next week and thereafter with them. They were Brother Clyde Farnes and his future wife, Kathy, and a Brother Terry (his last name I do not recall) and his future wife, Karen. These friendly couples made me feel welcome in America and in their ward.

It was very interesting and eye-opening to observe how the Church operated in a ward setting. Our little branch in Saigon had all the same ordinances and sang the same songs and taught the same things, but there were big differences. The ward had a piano and an organ to accompany the music, whereas in Saigon we started with only a baton to set the timing, and we didn't sing very well. We did eventually buy a piano. The Saigon Branch was in the habit of singing in English because the majority were Americans and about half of the Vietnamese spoke at least a little English. Translating the hymns was not then a priority. The Texas ward building was larger, of course, with many rows of ample bench seating. A microphone at the pulpit boomed out the messages of even the weakest voices. A gigantic folding wall at the back of the chapel could be either extended or closed as needed. Behind that wall was a beautiful and vast wood floor for dancing or playing, and beyond that there was a stage for the performances of plays. Two basketball hoops—I needed instructions as to their use—stood ready to entertain the youth. A full, modern kitchen was located just across the hall, ready to serve the needs of ward dinners and parties. Yes, it was the same Church, but it was surely not the same chapel. I wanted to shout to my American friends how fortunate they were, how exceedingly blessed they were in every way by the hand of God, but I said nothing of the sort. In quiet amazement, I just took it all in and dreamed of the day when such a magnificent structure might be built in my homeland for the use of the Saigon Saints. I was thrilled at the very thought. Someday, surely, it would come to pass.

At different points of my training, the U.S. Air Force provided its Vietnamese guests with some time away from school. To give us a glimpse of America beyond the base area, they took us on various excursions. Some were close at hand, like the Alamo in San Antonio. Not so close, but still in Texas, was the Houston Space Center, closely adjoining the Rice University campus. We saw the mission control room for the Apollo moon missions, a program that was still active at the time. We went to the visitors' center and viewed movies and saw exhibits. The technology involved in the moon missions was truly astounding to contemplate. So different was America from Vietnam, however, that I don't think visiting the moon from the earth was any more thrilling or mind-boggling to the astronauts than visiting America from Vietnam was to me.

Our language training group also went to Washington, D.C., to see the Pentagon, the central command post for U.S. military power. We rode on electric carts through the five-sided, three-ring-deep colossus complex and visited some of the generals involved with the war. We also visited the White House, the Capitol Building, the Washington Monument, the Lincoln and Jefferson Memorials, and the Smithsonian Institute. I believe the amazing thought for most foreigners visiting America, especially from civilizations thousands of years old, was, How did America become this prosperous and powerful in only two hundred years? In terms of time, that is nothing in Asia or compared to thousands of years of history in Egyptian, Near Eastern, or even some European cultures. Those cultures seemed to have almost frozen in time while America soared ahead of them all. Seeing America for myself proved to me that God's hand is surely upon the land of promise. The giant leap forward in America began around the time of the Restoration of the gospel. South Korea's giant leap came after the gospel was introduced there. Japan's giant leap came after the gospel was spread there. Will my homeland soar ahead? I wondered. Will the Saigon Branch be a stepping stone to a better future? My mind pondered these and many other questions. America is too big and too great to digest in one visit. Almost overwhelmed by these adventures, I was always content to return to my language studies in Texas.

The most significant events of my visit to the United States, however, had nothing to do with my language training. For instance, I received my patriarchal blessing while in Texas. My new LDS military friends asked me if I had such a blessing, and I said I did not. They helped me arrange to get one. I got my recommend for the blessing from my Texas bishop and made an appointment with the stake patriarch, Henry Eyring Turley. I wanted a blessing because I was very concerned at that time about my perceived inadequate abilities to translate important gospel truths into Vietnamese. I spent much of my off-duty time engaged in such translation work but did not have a strong confidence in my abilities. I think now I know why I had such feelings. The same adversary that teaches a man not to pray was perhaps trying to teach me not to translate. He discouraged me by telling me I wasn't skilled enough or deserving enough to be a translator. Patriarch Turley, who gave me my blessing on July 7, 1972, sensed this through the Spirit. In my blessing, I was blessed to have talents and abilities and leadership sufficient to help my people. I was blessed with the help of the Spirit in my work in the military. I was further blessed with the skills necessary to translate gospel material for the express purpose of helping to bring the gospel to the Vietnamese people. The mention of future blessings indicated to me that my life had a future and that I would be preserved through this time of war. I was grateful for my patriarchal blessing. It gave me an increased desire to be faithful in the gospel, as all these blessings were predicated upon my faithfulness.

I kept in contact with Lien every week by letter. As the time to deliver the new baby drew near at hand, I received no letters for three weeks. My concern grew considerably at that point. I became very concerned about her pregnancy and wondered if she was receiving the care she needed. My LDS friends suggested that I go to the American Red Cross for assistance, which I did. The Red Cross contacted Vietnam and by some means located my wife. That same evening, the Red Cross called and informed me that my wife had delivered a new baby boy. Everything was suddenly wonderful again! Now Tay had *two* sons! What a proud father I was! How grateful I was for the new assurances I derived from my patriarchal blessing. I felt that the Lord would bless us so that my sons would not be deprived of their father. I felt that Lien and

I would be the family I had hoped for when she was first being taught the gospel.

The American military had a provision to grant a short sabbatical leave for servicemen to attend a religious retreat or a major gathering of their faith. Brother Clyde and Brother Terry, the two servicemen who had taken me to Church and had helped me arrange to get my patriarchal blessing, were granted such an opportunity in 1972 to attend October general conference. They invited me to go with them to Salt Lake. This was an opportunity of a lifetime for me, but my school schedule conflicted with their proposed travel schedule. I prayed for God to open the door once again and let me enter. I had no reason to expect success in my request to be released early from my language studies, but I inquired nevertheless, as my schooling was nearly completed. The military authorities made an exception to their rules, and I was allowed to take my final exam a few days early. This blessing enabled me to complete my schooling in time to go to Salt Lake City for conference.

Due to our time constraints, we traveled straight through by car to Salt Lake. It took twenty-four hours to make the trip. We stopped only for gas, food, and bathroom breaks. Weary but thankful, we finally arrived safely in Salt Lake City. I was thrilled to realize I was in the city where prophets and apostles lived and where the headquarters of the Lord's restored Church was established. This was an amazing thing to someone who lived over five thousand miles away and had no means to travel on his own. It was another miracle.

One of my greatest dreams was realized as I viewed Temple Square, with its magnificent grounds and gardens surrounding the temple of granite that took forty years to construct. I was thrilled to sit in the Tabernacle at the feet of the Lord's prophet,

President Harold B. Lee, and the Apostles and other General Authorities. The glorious Tabernacle Choir sang the hymns of Zion like I had never heard them sung before. The sweet sound, absolutely heavenly, reverberated through my soul. How glorious it was to be in the presence of over seven thousand members of the Church, all under one big, domed roof. Thousands of others viewed the proceedings locally on television and listened on the radio. It was miraculous to me. I could scarcely believe my eyes as I gazed upon the Lord's living prophet and heard the words he spoke, as if from the Lord's own mouth. I feasted on the testimonies of all the speakers and soaked in the Spirit of the Lord in the meetings. A calming Spirit of complete gratitude swept over me. I only wished Lien and my sons could have shared in this time of spiritual renewal.

President Bradshaw's inspired prompting to give me a temple recommend before I left Saigon was validated. The two men who brought me to conference took me to the Salt Lake Temple and accompanied me during my first visit to the temple. They were most helpful to me and explained many matters pertaining to the temple and the ordinances therein. My thoughts were turned again to my parents and departed loved ones. I knew I must return someday and do their temple ordinances so that we could be sealed and together find the happiness that had eluded us for so long in this life. At that time, I reasoned with confidence, they will surely forgive me, and so might Ba, for not honoring their memory in the Buddhist manner. I also prayed that Lien would be baptized and partake of the gospel in its fullness. Since she was typing the translated scriptures for the translation committee, I prayed often that they might touch her heart as she did her work.

In celebration of my happy occasion of attending the temple and conference, and because my time in America was almost at an end, my Texas friends treated me to a special farewell dinner. We went to a fancy restaurant in Salt Lake City, and they ordered me a huge T-bone steak. It was so big! And so delicious! But, try as I might, I could not eat even one-third of it.

This big, delicious, expensive steak was symbolic to me of my entire experience in America. It is a country where the blessings are so great that none can partake of even a fraction of what's available. All Americans, even the poor ones, live better than the vast majority of people on this planet. Americans think nothing of turning a switch and getting light; turning a tap and getting water that is ample, clean, and pure, hot or cold, and delivered instantly without effort and upon demand; turning a key and taking their car on fine, paved roads wherever they choose to go. The bounteous blessings of God enjoyed in America are, like my T-bone steak, overwhelming to behold and impossible to fully partake.

After conference concluded, we drove straight through back to San Antonio. By the time we arrived, my fellow language students were gone. They had finished their schooling and checked out while I was away. The next day, I took a Greyhound bus from San Antonio to San Francisco. I rejoined my group at Travis Air Force Base just in time for our flight back to Vietnam. It was sobering to think that America is just one day away by jet aircraft from the turmoil, poverty, misery, and strife of my country or any other third-world country. How near, yet so far! The gulf between the daily lives of ordinary people in these two cultures seemed wider to me than the mighty Pacific Ocean.

As much as I loved America, I was very excited as the big U.S. Air Force transport plane rolled down the runway and slipped into the sky. As it passed over the California coastline, my excitement and anticipation increased. I sorely missed my home and my family and my friends in the Saigon Branch. I could see by the faces of the dozen or so American copassengers that they also sorely missed the homes and loved ones they left behind in order to help defend my country, which must have been especially difficult when so many soldiers were already being withdrawn. I silently prayed that they would all be like Samuel. This awkward combination of happy Vietnamese returning home and sullen Americans leaving home brought to mind a saying I heard in America that has an Asian equivalent: "One man's happiness is another man's misery." The tables would turn soon enough. The very aircraft that was taking me home would soon be jammed full of Americans returning to their homes as they rotated out of Vietnam, while somber Vietnamese would watch them leave and fret about the future. There was renewed cause for optimism, however. President Nixon's plan of gradual American troop withdrawals, coupled with the "Vietnamization" of the war—that is, increasingly turning the defense of South Vietnam over to the South Vietnamese—was almost complete. Secretary of State Henry Kissinger told the American people while I was at language school that "peace is at hand." I hoped with all my heart that he was right.

In any case, the "peace is at hand" prediction danced in my head. The war truly appeared to be nearing a close. The Paris Peace Talks had gone on for four years. It seemed like it took forever just for the parties to agree on the shape of the table where they met. President Nixon grew weary of the lack of progress and ordered the mining of Haiphong Harbor in

North Vietnam and increased the bombing of North Vietnamese positions. The North returned to the negotiating table with great haste, and concrete issues were finally resolved. Or seemed to be. The dream of peace, of all my dreams, was the one I wanted to come true first.

So it was that I returned to Saigon in October 1972 with great optimism that the war would end and the gospel would flourish. I was full of joy to see my wife and my son Vu and our new son. My wife had had full responsibility for caring for our family while I was away so long. She gave birth to our new baby, Huy (pronounced WHEE), with no husband to hold her hand and give her support. I thanked her for her sacrifice and love. It was hard for her to stay behind while I went off to school and enjoyed America. I greatly appreciated her support and told her so. I hoped we would never be separated for so long again. Now that we were reunited, I shared my experiences of the past six months in America. We had many things to be happy for. The branch was thriving, we had a healthy new son, my military position was safe, we had extra cash from my meal allowance, and the war was winding down. Everything seemed brighter and more hopeful than at any time for many years. The Saigon Saints and most Vietnamese people appeared to share my new sense of optimism.

CHAPTER 6

Departure of Military—Arrival of Missionaries

Everyone in the branch showed great interest in hearing of my adventures in the United States. Cao Minh and I compared our memories. He had received training in Mississippi almost ten years prior to my trip, but our impressions were much the same. I was saddened to be reminded by my wiser and older friend that "peace was at hand" back then as well. The only certain thing at hand when Mr. Kissinger made that statement was the U.S. presidential election in November 1972.

While I was away, the Saigon Branch had moved to a large, rented French villa next to the Chinese High School at Cho-Lon, the Chinese section of Saigon. It was there, on January 30, 1973, that my prayers concerning my wife were answered. That is the day I baptized Lien into The Church of Jesus Christ of Latter-day Saints. My prayers for her had been heard as she worked as a typist for the translation committee. Lien said she felt the Spirit as she typed the translated word of the Lord into Vietnamese and that she came to know the words were true. On the occasion of one of President Bradshaw's visits to the branch, she requested her baptism. I was exceedingly happy that she took this important step because it was necessary before we could ever be sealed in the house of the Lord. To kneel across the altar from Lien in the temple and have our marriage sealed for eternity and then to have our children sealed to us by one having authority to do so was one of my constant objectives and fondest dreams. For the past six years, it had seemed impossible to me that I would ever see a temple, given my situation and the distance of temples from my homeland. Now I knew, since I had gone to the house of the Lord, that all things are possible with God's help. I now believed firmly that someday my family would also enter those sacred walls with me. For the present, just seeing Lien join me in full fellowship with the Saigon Saints as a baptized member of the Church brought me great happiness.

In March 1973 I was called by President Bradshaw to head the translation committee. In addition to Sister Vy and Cao Minh, the committee included Brothers Dinh Van Thinh, Thai Que Liem, and Dang Van Hien, as well as Mr. Nguyen Khang and Mr. Phan Chanh Van. Since its beginning in the early sixties, the Saigon Branch had seen the need to translate not only basic pamphlets, but also the Book of Mormon, Doctrine and Covenants, and Pearl of Great Price into Vietnamese. Until the translation committee in Vietnam was formed in 1969 by direction of the First Presidency, there was no sustained and organized effort to do so. In the search for a translator to head the work, the Church had hired the brightest, most educated linguists available, including one holding a PhD from Columbia University, and had them translate a few pages of the Book of Mormon. The Translation Services Department analyzed the linguists' work and found it to be nearly a word-for-word translation that lacked the feeling and intent of the book. Based partly on her previous translation of "Joseph Smith's Testimony," they decided Sister Vy should lead the work.

When she was first selected to translate the Book of Mormon, Sister Vy approached the task with humility and soberness. She purchased a home in the countryside about ten miles from the branch that had the peace and solitude she sought to translate. Sister Vy translated most of the Book of Mormon at this country retreat. Cao Minh, myself, and others assisted her and edited the pages as she completed them and also edited the final manuscript, but Sister Vy was the primary translator. As she had done on her first pamphlet, Sister Vy read the Book of Mormon through several times in English and then translated by the Spirit. Surely the Lord preserved and prepared her for this very purpose.

The Bible was already available in Vietnamese. We on the committee also worked to translate missionary tracts and important books such as *A Marvelous Work and a Wonder* by LeGrand Richards. With the growth of our Vietnamese members and the great potential for missionary work among them, we felt increased urgency to move ahead with these projects.

The growing branch needed more space. There was renewed talk of building our own chapel. Cao Minh and I had seen firsthand the chapels of the American Saints and were united in our hope for a chapel of our own. At that time, the Bien Hoa Group had the only LDS-owned chapel in Vietnam. It was built in 1965 by LDS servicemen stationed at Bien Hoa Air Base, the base I had sometimes been charged with protecting during my combat days. The servicemen had paid for the chapel entirely with their own donations and by bartering their labor on other construction projects for surplus materials. It probably came as a great surprise to the LDS Church Building Committee in Salt Lake City when they found out they had a chapel in Vietnam for which they had extended no approval and expended no funds! It was of simple design, with backless benches for seating. But it was theirs. The faithful Brother Thach, a member of the Bien Hoa Group, received the gospel there through the efforts of American servicemen and my friend Cao Minh. If we had our own chapel, we could grow enough to fill it. Of this we were confident.

At the time I returned from America, there was continuing deliberation behind the scenes as to whether to send full-time missionaries to Vietnam. After all, Elder Hinckley had set the land apart for the preaching of the gospel in 1966. Mormon military missionaries had taught the gospel to many of their comrades and brought some Vietnamese associates into the Church. Now, due to the general withdrawal, the LDS military presence was dwindling fast. Full-time missionaries were being considered to carry on and expand the work the LDS military started.

What the LDS military members had accomplished as they mixed guns and the gospel was remarkable. They reached out to old members and brought in new ones. I am thankful for all those who planted the first gospel seeds in my homeland and bore the first fruit. Their methods were unorthodox at times, but they were effective.

One LDS army major, Stanley Schultz, was stationed at Tan Son Nhut Air Base. He was upset with the graffiti on the jeep he was assigned to drive, so he cleaned it up and gave it a new look. He painted in big letters below the jeep's windshield the name "Mahonri Moriancumer." This "brother of Jared" reference generated much interest. Major Schultz sought to attract members of the Church from out of the crowds of

BIEN HOA LDS SERVICEMEN'S GROUP AT CHAPEL, JULY 1971
(photograph courtesy Virgil N. Kovalenko)

LDS SERVICEMEN'S GROUP SACRAMENT MEETING, DECEMBER 1971
(photograph courtesy Gordon H. Weed)

FIRST THREE VIETNAMESE CONVERTS, SAIGON, EASTER, MARCH 29, 1964
LEFT TO RIGHT: Dang Thi Phuc, Nguyen Kim Huong, Cung Thi Hao
(photograph courtesy Clinton H. Gillmore)

MEMBER MISSIONARY JEEP "MAHONRI MORIANCUMER,"
TAN SON NHUT AIR BASE, SAIGON, 1970
(photograph courtesy Joachim Ed Scholz)

servicemen so he could inform them of where and when the Mormons met. He was successful in that endeavor. He also instilled a curiosity in some nonmembers that led to further gospel discussions.

Some LDS servicemen groups had unique reactivation programs to swell their numbers for Sunday services. There were in those days enterprising young Mormon officers with access to helicopters, especially on Sundays. On Sundays, these gospel leaders in search of a congregation flew to remote base camps in the field of battle. Sometimes they knew where to find Mormons, and other times they searched as led by the Spirit. In one camp after another, they found an LDS soldier here and another there. They "procured" all soldiers with *LDS* on their dog tags and ordered them onto the chopper. "Where are we going?" they would ask with trepidation. "To church!" was the reply. Off they went to fellowship and reconnect with the gospel of Jesus Christ. When they returned later in the day, many were strengthened and comforted by the experience.

One concerned Latter-day Saint soldier, Chaplain Terry Baker, frequently collected LDS boys from the LBJ on Sunday mornings. No, it wasn't President Lyndon B. Johnson's LBJ Ranch; it was the Long Binh Jail. The infamous jail was generally overflowing after a Saturday night of drinking, carousing, and fighting. Sadly, but predictably, there were usually a few amnesiac Mormons in the mix who had forgotten who they were. This gospel hero secured their freedom, extended the hand of fellowship, and took them to church. Because someone cared, some took their first steps back to the straight and narrow path from which they had wandered.

Another LDS soldier, told by his commander that he could not wear his white nonregulation underwear, dyed his temple garments green rather than part with them. He stood before an LDS servicemen's group, wearing his green garments beneath his clothes, and bore solemn testimony of the protection they provided him not only from the bullets of battle but from the fiery darts of the adversary. The power of his words and example brought battle-tested men to tears.

How could I not love and appreciate such men? My own introduction to the gospel and that of my friend Cao Minh and so many others had come through LDS members of the American military. When the Vietnamese encountered an LDS American who was kind and respectful and whose language and behavior were commendable, they became curious because such soldiers were not the norm. They would ask, "Why are you so different?" The question was often answered with the "golden questions." In their own way, they would ask, "What do you know about the Mormon Church?" and "Would you like to know more?" Soon, in Vietnam, at least, their opportunities to ask such questions would cease.

On January 1, 1973, the Paris Peace Accord was signed. The hostilities were set to end. A condition of the treaty was that the Americans must leave Vietnam within sixty days. All of the LDS servicemen's groups would be dissolved. Unless something was done, when the LDS soldiers departed, the missionary program in Vietnam would leave with them. The discussion as to whether to send in the full-time elders resumed with added urgency among leaders of the Church. President Bradshaw was already being prepared to offer his opinion in the matter.

President Bradshaw's first visit to Vietnam with the outgoing Hong Kong mission president, Brent Hardy, was in 1971. From that time to 1973, he observed the increase in the numbers of Vietnamese members and the decrease in LDS servicemen as the gradual withdrawal progressed. He recognized the need to carry on the work the LDS military had started and began laying the groundwork for full-time missionaries.

President Bradshaw met with the Vietnamese attorney who had helped obtain legal status for the Church in Vietnam back in 1967. He obtained documents certifying the Church's legal status and that it had the right to own property in Vietnam. He inquired of Ellsworth Bunker, the American ambassador to Vietnam, as to the legal and safety concerns the Church might need to address should missionaries be sent to Saigon. President Bradshaw also had knowledgeable LDS contacts in the U.S. military, former Hong Kong missionaries, who kept him apprised of the relative safety around Saigon. He began suggesting to visiting Church leaders that full-time missionaries be sent to Vietnam. He received enough encouragement that in March 1972 he wrote a letter to President Marion G. Romney and laid out the case for sending in the missionaries. President Bradshaw said later, "This was one of the most poorly timed letters ever written. On the same day President Romney received the letter on his desk, the national news reported increased hostilities so great and peace prospects so grim that he didn't even bother sending a reply." President Bradshaw remained convinced, even though the idea was temporarily placed on the back burner in Salt Lake.

In November 1972 the American ambassador to Vietnam sent a reply to President Bradshaw's questions. Ambassador Bunker believed that missionaries, if sent, would be as safe or safer in Saigon as in any other large Asian city where missionaries were currently laboring. He also answered some legal questions favorably.

Elder Gordon B. Hinckley pondered the fact that all the LDS servicemen were leaving Saigon. He had missionary responsibilities for the area that included Vietnam and wrote to President Bradshaw and basically asked two questions, "What are you going to do when the servicemen leave?" and "What is going to happen to the branch in Saigon?" President Bradshaw, aware of Elder Hinckley's great interest and love for the Vietnamese Saints, wanted to respond to the inquiry but did not know the answer to his satisfaction. Nevertheless, he was asked to send his recommendations to Elder Hinckley. In February 1973 he decided to go to the top of the Caravelle Hotel in downtown Saigon, the same spot where Elder Hinckley had dedicated the land for missionary work, and there President Bradshaw inquired of the Lord. President Bradshaw's strong impression after his prayer was that the missionaries should be sent to Vietnam and that the Saigon Branch would grow. He didn't know what would happen for sure but felt that the missionaries could do well as long as they were there. He also felt that the missionaries would be protected and that the Church didn't need to worry about their safety. He had LDS contacts in the intelligence community that monitored the whereabouts of the North Vietnamese forces and was confident they would have ample warning if they had to leave. Admittedly, sending in the full-time missionaries was contrary to normal procedures. The Church tends to evacuate missionaries from troubled areas, not send them in. Nevertheless, President Bradshaw wrote to Elder Hinckley and restated his case for sending missionaries to Saigon.

A few weeks later, President Bradshaw received a letter dated March 13, 1973, from the First Presidency and the Quorum of the Twelve giving him permission to assign some missionaries to the mission. President Bradshaw was so excited he shouted for joy and immediately spread the good news in the mission home; he didn't immediately read the complete letter. There were several conditions. One condition was that he needed permission from the parents of the missionaries he selected. He had plenty of volunteers to choose from. A few even offered some missionary humor, saying they would go if they could be Demilitarized Zone Leaders. Humor aside, many were enthusiastically willing to serve if selected.

President Bradshaw asked for and received parental permission and made his selections. The parents of each missionary expressed concern about the dangers but placed their faith in the Lord. They also noted their sons' confident and yearning pleas to allow them to accept this opportunity. The first four full-time missionaries sent to Vietnam were Elders Colin Van Orman, James Christensen, David Posey, and Richard Holloman. President Bradshaw selected April 6, 1973, to take the missionaries to Vietnam. The Saigon Branch threw a big welcoming party for the newly arrived missionaries. All the members and some investigators, obviously overjoyed to have them, provided a traditional Vietnamese celebratory dinner for the elders at the branch. They excitedly showered the elders with thanks and good wishes and offers to help. The Saigon Saints were truly thrilled that the Church sent the missionaries into Vietnam. It restored their hope in the branch's future, the hope that had dwindled somewhat during the removal of the American military. The missionaries' presence signaled to the Saigon Saints that the Church intended for the branch to continue to grow and prosper as before, only better.

After the very warm welcome, the elders retired to their quarters for instruction from President Bradshaw. The first four elders lived in two bedrooms behind the branch chapel, part of the large French villa. As more missionaries arrived, additional quarters were found. On that first night, President

Bradshaw, in the privacy of their new quarters, gave much instruction, warning, and counsel to the elders. They knelt together in prayer. One might think that after the meeting the group would have been given to a somber mood. But any feelings of apprehension gave way to the exhilaration and thrill of being part of the history and happiness of the moment. They were so happy, in fact, that they spontaneously gathered in one big group hug and laughed out loud as they jumped up and down like little children. It was a fitting beginning on the occasion of the full-time missionaries commencing their labors in Vietnam.

The next day, President Bradshaw showed the missionaries around town and took them to the rooftop garden room of the Caravelle Hotel. He spoke about Elder Hinckley's dedicatory prayer there and also of his own plea for guidance on the matter of assigning full-time missionaries to Saigon. Now, here they were, overlooking Saigon, a city of over two million souls. The missionaries were enthusiastic and ready to thrust in the sickle and begin the harvest. They prayed on the roof and felt the Spirit in abundance. Strangely, they were not full of fear. The city felt safe to them, even though it looked like a war zone. Machine gun nests and barbed-wire barriers were at every intersection, and certain areas of the city were off-limits. President Bradford warned the missionaries to avoid unsafe parts of the city, the areas infested with brothels, black markets, seedy bars, and dangerous characters. He also realized that some Vietnamese were angry because America's military had contributed to the moral decline of the city. Others were angry because the Americans left before peace was secured. There were also many young children, amputees missing arms or legs, selling cigarettes on the streets of Saigon for their survival. Abandoned mixed-race Amerasian children wandered

PRESIDENT WILLIAM S. AND SISTER MARJORIE BRADSHAW ON TOP OF
CARAVELLE HOTEL WITH THREE OF THE FIRST FOUR MISSIONARIES IN VIETNAM
LEFT TO RIGHT: President Bradshaw, Elder David T. Posey, Sister Bradshaw, Elder Richard C. Holloman,
Elder Colin Van Orman. The fourth missionary, Elder James L. Christensen, took the picture.

(photograph courtesy James L. Christensen)

VIEW FROM CARAVELLE HOTEL OVERLOOKING SAIGON, 1987
(photograph courtesy Virgil N. Kovalenko)

FIRST FOUR MISSIONARIES TO SERVE IN VIETNAM STANDING IN FRONT OF THE
SAIGON BRANCH CHAPEL AND ELDERS' RESIDENCE, APRIL 1973
LEFT TO RIGHT: Elders James L. Christensen, Richard C. Holloman, David T. Posey, Colin Van Orman
(photograph courtesy James L. Christensen)

SAIGON BRANCH SACRAMENT MEETING, APRIL 1973
(photograph courtesy James L. Christensen)

the streets, homeless and shunned by both races. Some blamed Americans for their maimed and dead as much as they did the communist invaders from the North. President Bradshaw was aware that this resentment for Americans, however misplaced and however widespread, might make the missionaries targets for someone's idea of revenge. Still, as they descended from the roof of the Caravelle Hotel, the missionaries were full of faith and purpose. The missionaries felt that if they obeyed the mission rules President Bradshaw outlined for them, the Lord would be willing to protect them. Time proved them right.

On Sunday, April 8, 1973, President Bradshaw reorganized the Saigon Branch and set me apart as the new branch president. One of a handful of remaining American priesthood holders was called as my first counselor. Dr. Lester Bush was an LDS medical doctor attached to the U.S. embassy. He and his wife, Yvonne, spent many hours of devoted service in the branch. The American members had always filled most of the leadership positions in the branch and were well respected and were looked to for guidance. Brother and Sister Bush were extraordinarily devoted to the gospel, and they gave me much needed help and advice as I assumed my new duties. Dr. Bush also provided medical services for the missionaries when needed. My other counselor was Brother Dang Thong Nhat, a young unmarried man, twenty-four years old, with whom I had served in the former presidency and who was very bright and helpful as well. When Dr. Bush left about a year later, Le Van Kha, my old and trusted friend, was called as second counselor, and Brother Nhat became first counselor.

It seemed for us a whole new beginning for the branch. With the new missionaries in place and our old ties with LDS servicemen severed, it was with great hope and humility and considerable anxiety that I accepted my call to lead the Saigon Branch.

President Bradshaw returned to Hong Kong, and the missionaries got down to business. The translation committee had already prepared several missionary pamphlets, but the elders did not yet know Vietnamese; they spoke Chinese. They immediately set out to learn the Vietnamese language. The missionaries hired a branch member named Pauline Bin to teach them Vietnamese. For the next few months, they met with her each morning on the porch of the villa and soon learned the Vietnamese language. Sister Bin was Chinese but also spoke English, French, and Vietnamese. The missionaries found they learned Vietnamese more quickly when being taught from a Chinese perspective. Since they already knew Chinese, which is closely related to Vietnamese, Sister Bin's lessons "clicked" better than when they were taught in English. I marveled at the wisdom of the Lord, which so often confounds the understanding of men. Americans were taught Vietnamese in Chinese and promptly learned it almost perfectly.

Even as they learned the language, there was much work to do. Now that the American members were mostly gone, it seemed silly to continue singing our hymns in English, but none of the hymns were translated. The missionaries requested that the hymns be translated so they could be sung in our native tongue. The first song we translated was "Love at Home." While other hymns and projects were being worked on, for about a month we sang "Love at Home" for the opening song, "Love at Home" for the sacrament song, and "Love at Home" for the closing song.

Each Sunday afternoon following church, the missionaries worked with the translation committee as we prepared and refined tracts and pamphlets for their use and translated more of the hymns of Zion into Vietnamese. They also helped us in matters of doctrine as we tried to translate gospel principles from one language to another. They helped ensure that nothing of importance was lost in the translation. They also discussed any problems they had observed during the week with the members' understanding of the gospel. For instance, the role of women in Vietnamese culture was viewed as less prominent than in the Church. A lesson on the equality and importance of the roles of parents and spouses might be suggested. The missionaries visited with leaders of other Christian faiths in Saigon and obtained useful Christian pamphlets in Vietnamese. They also purchased Vietnamese Bibles, which they utilized in teaching about the Savior.

The Vietnamese government had restrictions on soliciting door to door, so the missionaries developed other methods. Partly to become familiar with the area, the missionaries rode the public buses to the end of the different bus lines and back. On the buses, they met many curious Vietnamese citizens who inquired about the nature of their work. When told they were missionaries, some took an interest. In those early days, the missionaries got the names and addresses of potential investigators and told them they would come see them when they could speak better Vietnamese. Their progress in speaking was nothing short of remarkable. Surely the Lord gave them the gift of tongues, for they were speaking in excellent Vietnamese before four months passed. Their skills were such that on the telephone, the Vietnamese mistook some of them for native speakers.

Perhaps the missionaries' favorite method of attracting potential investigators was to stand on a busy street corner in Saigon and hold up a map of the city and project a puzzled look upon their faces. Friendly Vietnamese citizens saw their map, assumed they were lost, and offered their assistance. They sometimes walked with the missionaries to their destination. By the end of the walk, the missionaries often made appointments for gospel discussions. Dozens of these map encounters led to baptisms.

The missionaries also worked with the nonmembers among the families who had already joined the Church. The parents and siblings of Saigon Branch members often attended meetings and activities as investigators. At times, we had nearly as many investigators as members at our meetings, so the missionaries didn't have to look far for people to teach.

Another source of referrals came from faraway Salt Lake City. As LDS veterans who had served in Vietnam and visiting Vietnamese citizens toured Temple Square, they filled out referral cards for friends and relatives in Vietnam. The missionaries received hundreds of such referrals and followed up on as many as could be located in Saigon.

The first four missionaries who found themselves in Saigon must have agreed that the Lord works in mysterious ways. Their mission calls had all indicated that they were going to learn Chinese and go to Hong Kong, and they did. But the fact that they ended up in Vietnam speaking Vietnamese was amazing to them. They served with all their hearts and are remembered with love to this day by the former Saigon Branch members. For safety reasons, the missionaries initially traveled in a single group. Later, when they became known to the local residents and enjoyed respect for their courage and devotion, they traveled throughout the capital in pairs. As some missionaries left when their missions ended, more were assigned. After the first missionaries baptized dozens of new members in the first few months, other missionaries in the Hong Kong Mission started campaigning for President Bradshaw to send them to Vietnam. Over the next two years, twelve more were added. A total of fifteen missionaries came to Vietnam before the fall of Saigon. As many as ten were there at the same time. (In addition to the original four elders, the other missionaries were Corey D. Anderson, Richard S. Bowman, Derrell S. Elmer, Dale B. Guest, Milton Harris, Blaine L. Hart, Lewis A. Hassell, Benjamin F. Jones, Marvin Labrie, Dee Oviatt, and Robert Collette.)

Each of the first four missionaries was given a Vietnamese nickname by the people of the Saigon Branch. Many of us could not pronounce the American names very well, so we affectionately renamed them with Vietnamese names that rolled off our tongues with ease. These nicknames were well received, and the practice continued as each of the other groups arrived.

The first missionaries called specifically to Vietnam were Corey Anderson and Dee Oviatt. They arrived in December 1973. Dee Oviatt told me of his mother's reaction to the unexpected destination of his call. In Dee's family, his mother cheered everyone with the spirit of "I'll go where you want me to go, dear Lord." She had anxiously awaited an end to the American involvement in Vietnam and had prayed for years, almost obsessively, that her son would not be sent there as a soldier. Now the Americans were out and her prayers were answered, sort of. Her prayers should have been more specific. "Can you imagine her shock," said Brother Oviatt, "when she read that my mission call to the Hong Kong Mission indicated I would serve in Vietnam? She gasped in disbelief and nearly fainted. She almost refused to let me go." But he did go, and he served faithfully to the end. He and Elder Richard S. Bowman, in fact, were the last ones to leave.

The fact that I had been to America and that I spoke English was a great help to me and to the missionaries as they began their work. I could understand what they had left behind to come teach the gospel in a far-off land. I could understand the anxiety of parents and loved ones who prayed for their safe return. I did my best to help them in their labors and familiarize them with the culture. Everyone did.

Besides my first counselor, Dr. Bush, a few other LDS Americans still lived in the branch. Mel Madsen was a civilian contractor in the construction business who had diplomatic status. He was a favorite of the missionaries because while he was at work all day, he left his house open for them to rest and recuperate from the heat and physical demands of their labors. He always left a plate of cookies out for them and stocked his refrigerator with milk and food. Brother William C. Miner was also involved in the construction business. He had married a Vietnamese woman and adopted her children. They were active members of the branch and were also helpful in teaching language and customs. Another faithful branch member was Brother George Reading. I believe he was the last American member to leave Saigon. He worked for a large shipping company and departed Vietnam by ship bound for Singapore, where he remained working for his company rather than returning to America.

Sister Vy, noted for her pleasant manners and social grace, also helped the missionaries greatly in learning Vietnamese customs and culture. The missionaries returned Sister Vy's favor by opening up English classes to the public, a thing Sister Vy desired. Soon, more than one hundred students were attending the classes two or three times a week. Invitations to hear about the gospel were extended. Besides learning a valuable skill, one that Sister Vy very much wanted to impart to others, many students were baptized as a result of the English classes.

MEL MADSEN
(photograph courtesy Leo Loving)

SISTER VY WITH GIRLS OF THE SAIGON BRANCH YWMIA, ABOUT 1969–70
(photograph courtesy of VASAA archives)

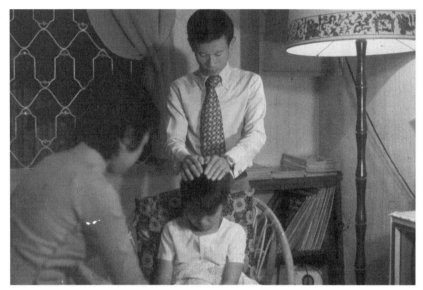

PRESIDENT TAY GIVING SPECIAL BLESSING TO SISTER-IN-LAW LOAN LE, 1973
(photograph courtesy James L. Christensen)

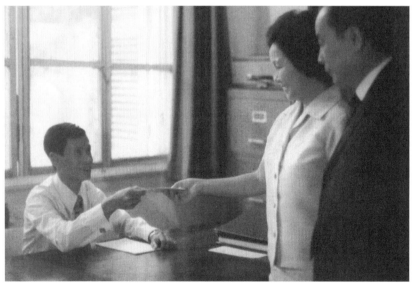

PRESIDENT TAY RECEIVES TITHING FROM SAIGON BRANCH MEMBERS
(courtesy of The Van Nguyen)

The branch steadily reached new milestones of membership. Elder Van Orman reported to President Bradshaw that in April 1973 when they arrived, the first branch meeting had 23 Vietnamese and 21 Americans in attendance. One year later, he reported that there were 140 Vietnamese and 15 Americans in the branch. Unfortunately, as we progressed in the branch, the advancing army from the North also progressed and moved ever closer to Saigon. Many brethren, including some in branch leadership, were reassigned to duty in the new war zones outside of the city and could no longer attend branch meetings. The high hopes generated by the Paris Peace Talks began to fade.

When an entire family joined the Church at once, it was a significant event in our branch. Besides there not being a lot of complete families to teach in the first place, there was a problem with tradition. There is an ingrained notion in Vietnamese society that youth are not as important as the older heads of families. To have young men conducting services and presiding over their elders in the Church was an awkward situation for investigators to observe. They felt it was disrespectful and offensive, and older family members would often cease their investigations immediately. After the Americans left, we had too few priesthood holders to properly staff the leadership positions in the Saigon Branch. Sister Vy's Relief Society sisters greatly outnumbered our men in the priesthood. We were trying to operate our branch as any other in the Church, and to be successful, we knew we needed more complete families. The missionaries sought to balance the branch by baptizing more men, along with their families, and thereby increase the number of priesthood holders. The missionaries' new emphasis on teaching complete families was successful and quickly balanced our needs. The entire Tuan family of seven was one of the first baptized, but more would follow in the two years the missionaries were there. The last complete family, the Doans, a family of twelve, joined the Church just a month before the collapse of the branch. Even before that time, Vietnamese members filled all of the offices in the branch. We felt good about our progress and were excited about the possibilities unfolding before us.

The Saigon Branch was growing at a rate that prompted us to consider once again purchasing land for a chapel. By 1973 we were ready to buy a piece of property upon which to build a chapel. We wanted to build something tangible to serve as a testimony to our faith and commitment. Moreover, we wished to show the Lord our gratitude and our dedication to sharing the gospel. Our hope and dream was that building such a chapel would be the beginning of spreading the gospel of peace across the land.

Except for the servicemen's chapel at Bien Hoa, the Church still had no buildings in Vietnam. With the Americans gone, the Bien Hoa chapel was just waiting for a congregation. When two more missionaries arrived in Saigon in early 1974, they went to Bien Hoa Air Base and reestablished contact with Nguyen Ngoc Thach and his family. The missionaries were excited about the chapel and envisioned it as a headquarters for future missionary activity in that area. The government, however, declared the area unsafe for holding religious services, and the chapel was never used again.

Undaunted, we pressed on in our attempt to obtain our own chapel. The LDS servicemen in Vietnam had left us a great gift. There was a special fund established for us in Vietnam with which to build a future chapel. During the course of American involvement in the war, over 1,500 LDS servicemen donated one month of combat pay each (about sixty-five dollars) to the LDS Church building fund earmarked for the Vietnamese Saints. There was over a hundred thousand dollars in the fund, and with this wonderful gift we intended to build our chapel. First, we looked around for suitable property on which to build. We looked at several lots, and when President Bradshaw visited, he would counsel us on each lot. Too often, for one reason or another, the property was not compatible with our needs or something was not right with the terms of purchase. Our disappointment over these problems was great, but we continued to grow and function as a branch and look for a place to build our chapel. Late in 1974 our membership topped two hundred.

The growth of the branch since the missionaries' arrival was truly impressive to all of us. The very presence of the missionaries was a source of strength and comfort for the Saigon Saints. We all shared the space under their umbrella of protection. As long as the missionaries labored in Saigon, we thought, the tides of war would be held back. All the while, preparations for war were everywhere. The young missionaries moved about the city, passing many armaments and fortified positions to reach the destinations where they could teach the gospel. The missionaries were also fortified with the full armor of God. They needed such protection. As President Bradshaw had anticipated, they sometimes encountered disgruntled and angry Vietnamese who hurled verbal insults and obscene gestures at them as they passed by, simply because they were Americans. There was a distinct contrast between these young messengers of the Lord, armed only with their scriptures, making themselves easy targets with white shirts and ties, and the heavily armed sandbag bunkers and barbed-wire encampments they walked beside. Somehow, just having them in Saigon gave us hope that we would be preserved against the enemy. We felt that the armies of heaven would fight the battles of our little band of Saints and prevent us from perishing. Perhaps there was never a little branch more faithful or hopeful than we were. For the two years the missionaries labored among us there was war all around, but it stayed away for a season, and the missionaries courageously performed their labors.

I continued as branch president and as head of the translation committee during all this time. In May 1974, when the Book of Mormon transcript was completed and ready to be reviewed by the Translation Services Department in Salt Lake, President Bradshaw made forty or fifty copies of the manuscript for the judicious use of the missionaries, branch members, and investigators. He sent the original to the Translation Service Department to prepare it for publication. Even though we did not yet have an official published version with an index and cross-references, the work by Sister Vy and others was complete as to the content of the book itself. Having these scriptures available in the Vietnamese language strengthened many testimonies.

CHAPTER 7

The Dream Unravels

In July 1974, President Bradshaw was replaced by President Jerry D. Wheat. He continued to support sending additional missionaries to Saigon. He visited Saigon every two or three weeks to counsel the missionaries and conduct business in the branch. Almost as often as President Wheat visited, we would impose on him to look at yet another property to evaluate and hopefully approve for purchase. One property in particular seemed perfect for us, and we were at the point of closing the purchase. The seller wanted some payment in Vietnamese money and some in other currency. President Wheat looked at the property and liked it very much, but the Spirit told him we did not have all the facts. He asked Elder Bowman to check into the matter more carefully before anyone signed any papers. Confident we would learn the truth, he returned to Hong Kong. We were upset with this setback until it was discovered the seller did not reveal an easement that took up over one-third of the property. The property we negotiated in good faith to buy was suddenly rendered unsuitable when we learned that a clear title could not be transferred. Without an assurance of full ownership, we could not risk building on the ground. We were heartbroken but wiser from the experience. President Wheat saved the sacrifice of the servicemen, their combat pay donations, from falling into the hands of an unscrupulous seller. The money remained in safekeeping for use at some future time because of his inspiration.

For the Saigon Branch and for the country of South Vietnam, things began to unravel quickly early in April 1975. Even as hostilities increased and the communist forces inched ever closer to Saigon, President Wheat resisted removing the missionaries for as long as possible, but finally it could not be avoided. On April 2, 1975, all but two of the missionaries were recalled to Hong Kong by President Wheat, just two years from the time the first missionaries arrived. Their protection, and ours, was his top concern. Elders Dee Oviatt and Richard Bowman were the last to leave, on April 4, 1975. Before they left, the missionaries and I hauled away and burned all Church-related materials in the branch so they couldn't be used against us if the branch building fell into the hands of the communists. As an exception, and as a precaution, I held back several copies each of the translated materials we had. They were hand carried out of Vietnam by Elders Oviatt and Bowman on April 4.

It seemed impossible that the last of the missionaries were gone. So much had been accomplished by so few in such a short time. Because of the love and fellowship they had established with the Saints in Vietnam, the departure of the full-time missionaries was a very emotional event indeed. The umbrella of protection that hovered over them was something we did not wish to lose. They were simply irreplaceable. There was still so much to do. Some people were ready for baptism; many others were anxious to be taught. Oh, how sad I was to say good-bye to them! While some Saints felt they had been deserted, most of us realized that the missionaries were simply too easy a target for the communists if the worst should come. Some of the missionaries even protested going, but they had to leave for their own safety. We all hoped it was just a temporary precaution until the war wound down a bit. That was just more wishful thinking.

On April 5, 1975, I sent my final report for the translation committee to Brother Watanabe in Tokyo. I advised him that multiple copies of all the translated materials in my stewardship had been sent out of Vietnam with the departing missionaries and by other means to ensure their preservation. I reported that all English-language pamphlets and other Church materials had been burned. Previously, the branch membership records had been hand carried out of the country by President Jerry Wheat and Elders Oviatt and Bowman. They were immediately put to good use. Within a week, they had prepared a list of branch members for the American consulate in Hong Kong to be cabled to the U.S. embassy in Saigon for use in a possible evacuation.

In Washington, President Ford was greatly concerned about the six thousand American embassy and civilian workers still in Vietnam and the tens of thousands of Vietnamese with American ties whose lives were in grave peril if the communists prevailed. He said in an address to a joint session of Congress on April 10, 1975, that the United States had a profound moral obligation to these people. "The situation in South Vietnam is changing rapidly. . . . Fundamental decency requires that we do everything in our power to ease the misery and pain of the monumental human crisis which has fallen on the people of Vietnam." The White House dilemma was that if Ford moved too quickly to evacuate the Americans, the Thieu government of South Vietnam would collapse and possibly set off an anti-American panic in Saigon. If he waited too long, the remaining U.S. citizens would be engulfed in the collapse and many possibly killed by panicking South Vietnamese or attacking North Vietnamese. On April 14, President Ford asked Congress for authority to evacuate 176,000 South Vietnamese and by the next day $200 million was tentatively approved to finance the evacuation. All the while, in Vietnam, rumors of the U.S. Marines returning to South Vietnam persisted. There was talk of mercy missions to save the faltering South Vietnamese armed forces. While unfounded, this kind of speculation gave us hope.

It was during this time that the weight of my calling as branch president began to feel very heavy. The Saints began to feel abandoned and day by day became more concerned over their fate. Neighboring Cambodia had already fallen to the communists. We had received reports that in Cambodia mass marches of refugees were fleeing the cities for the rural areas. We had heard of the death and misery that people in Cambodia had experienced because of the fall of their government. Such talk was exceedingly frightening to us.

The Saigon Saints looked to me to help them escape the tyranny we most certainly would face if our government fell. They looked to me to administer the affairs of the Church in Saigon as directed by President Wheat, who in turn took direction from the General Authorities. I was now nearly cut off from my higher authorities and advisers. I felt lower than low, but I was the highest Church authority in Vietnam. I am but a small man; the weight of responsibility was almost more than I could bear. I wanted to help calm the fears of the members and see their expressions of fear turn to hope and faith, but I was fearful also. I didn't know what I should do. I needed help and prayed for the Lord to send it. My prayers were answered when President Wheat and Elder Bowman suddenly returned from Hong Kong to prepare the way for a plan designed to allow the Saints to make an orderly departure.

On April 16, President Wheat told me of the list of members sent to the embassy. The next day we went to the embassy to verify that the list had arrived and that it was complete. Getting into the embassy was no easy task. Thousands of South Vietnamese were clamoring outside the gates of the embassy, trying to gain entrance by any means possible. "How will we get inside?" asked President Wheat. Elder Bowman took a business card from his wallet that was embossed "Ted Price, American Consulate" and held it up. It was like waving a magic wand. We were allowed to pass by the sentries guarding the way. President Wheat also had a letter of introduction from the U.S. consulate in Hong Kong. The panic and confusion outside the embassy was matched by the hysteria inside. Everyone was desperately seeking a way to leave Vietnam. We went from office to office looking for someone who knew about the list sent to them from the embassy in Hong Kong. Nobody seemed to know or care about the list. At last we met Mr. Jacobson, an embassy consul, who told us he didn't know anything about our list.

President Wheat persisted about the list, because David C. Hoopes, a son-in-law to Elder A. Theodore Tuttle and a special assistant to the president of the United States, had told him he had also sent a teletype of the branch list from Washington to the embassy in Saigon. President Wheat suggested calling Mr. Hoopes, and the consul said, "No! Even we would be arrested if we called the White House!" Finally, President Wheat convinced the high embassy official that he really did know Mr. Hoopes and it was in his interest to make the call. Being after midnight in Washington, David Hoopes was reached at his home. After talking to President Wheat for a moment, Brother Hoopes asked to speak to the embassy official, Mr. Jacobson. We don't know what Brother Hoopes was saying, but Mr. Jacobson was only listening and saying, "Yes, sir! Yes, sir!" a lot while the color drained from his face. When he was off the phone, Mr. Jacobson pointed in disgust to another room and said the list was there. He suggested we check it for accuracy. His coldness, even after a request from a member of the White House staff, suggested he wasn't going to help us. We checked the list for spelling and completeness. The list contained only members of the branch and some investigators but not their nonmember relatives. This was a problem we tried to correct but could not before time ran out. Before we left the embassy, some five hours after entering, we were introduced to someone who was instructed to help us. I was given a phone number and a contact man, Mr. Currier, to call twice a day for instructions so I would not have to fight the crowds to reenter the embassy. They would tell us when the evacuation started.

The reason it hadn't started already was that Congress had not yet finalized the appropriation to finance the evacuation. The evacuation plans were being made in secret in case funds were approved. Many corporations and private individuals were not waiting for the government plan to be worked out. They simply bought airline tickets for their key people and flew them out of the country. After the fact, some branch members wondered why the Church didn't make its own arrangements and fly us out commercially. I do not speak for the Church, but I think there were two reasons. First, the military men would need to desert their units, a crime punishable by death, and the Church did not want to promote desertion in the hour of need. Second, there was general uncertainty about the plans of the

North Vietnamese troops, and the Church probably felt there was plenty of time to go through proper government channels. The evacuation plan was a good plan from my point of view, and had it gone as planned, no one would have had anything to complain about. Whatever the reason, Church leaders outside Vietnam did not pursue an alternative to the government evacuation plan.

I felt there would be plenty of time for the plan to be successfully executed. Even if Saigon fell, most branch members speculated that it would take several months. Cities in Cambodia like Phnom Penh, with far fewer troops and defensive fortifications than Saigon, had taken months to fall. Surely Saigon, with all of its soldiers and armament, would take much longer than Phnom Penh to conquer. In the meantime, most Vietnamese thought that an outraged international community would come to our aid, especially after the terrible butchery in Cambodia, and that our freedom would be preserved. Within the branch, we felt that the gospel had blessed the lives of so many in recent months that we would be given more time to build up the Church in Vietnam. Everyone was wrong on all counts.

Before President Wheat and Elder Bowman left for Hong Kong for the last time, we held a special meeting at the branch. We did not dare tell the branch members that we had just given the U.S. embassy a list containing their names for possible evacuation. The South Vietnamese government was very strict, and great pressures could be brought upon us if it were known that we were participating in a contingency plan for an organized evacuation. During our meeting, held on April 17, President Wheat and I told the branch members that in the event of an emergency, we would try to arrange for their evacuation, but we did not disclose any specifics at that time.

This led some members to fill in the blanks themselves with any wild speculation they could conjure up.

During the meeting, I became the subject of a substantial amount of criticism. Some members accused me of hiding the whole truth from them (which I was). They accused me of planning to be secretly evacuated without them (which was not true). My heart was sad and very heavy when I heard the members accuse me in this manner, but I could not yet reveal what President Wheat and I had done earlier in the day. Even President Wheat felt our meeting was a heartbreaking experience. He was saddened to be where members had faith in their leaders but where the leaders could not reveal the tentative plan to save them from the communists. President Wheat counseled them to hang on, to have faith, to keep the commandments, and to love the Lord. He suggested they attend church services as long as they were able to do so and said that they would be kept informed of future developments. By the time the meeting ended, he became increasingly sick and heartbroken over the plight of the Saints there. I could see that the heavy weight that I felt was not entirely on my shoulders after all. It was clear that this was also a very emotional time for President Wheat. I noticed—and he confirmed—that he had lost about twenty-five pounds of weight in just a few weeks. This was no doubt because of his emotional stress, loss of appetite, and sleepless nights worrying about the Saigon Saints.

One incident fresh on President Wheat's mind was the case of branch member Tran Van Nhon, who so feared the coming fall of Saigon that he and his wife gave up their three children for adoption to a volunteer agency in Michigan. He and his wife felt that if their children escaped Vietnam through adoption, at least their lives would be saved and they could continue to grow up under the influence of the Church in a free America.

He tearfully pleaded with President Wheat to ensure that they could eventually know the location of their children and that they would be placed in an LDS home in Michigan. This experience and many others made the entire situation very heartbreaking for President Wheat, who had labored so hard in this part of the mission field.

On Friday, April 18, President Wheat and Elder Bowman prepared to return to Hong Kong. The North Vietnamese were within twenty miles of the city. Escape was becoming an appropriate word even for commercial flights. The airport, like the embassy, was ringed with a mass of humanity clamoring to leave. Without passports and proper papers, no one could enter the base, but desperate people stood around night and day waiting for a chance to somehow slip by guards or bribe their way in. Even as President Wheat and Elder Bowman said their final good-byes, shells and rockets could be heard hitting closer and closer to the city. In fact, the smell of gunpowder from exploding shells filled the air over Saigon, leaving an odor much like that of the millions of firecrackers set off in happier days at Tet celebrations. I bade a reluctant farewell to President Wheat and Elder Bowman and returned to my former status as the last and loneliest Church leader in Saigon.

The government, with insane desperation, ordered the entrances to the city closed to the streams of refugees coming in from the countryside to escape the advancing communists. Nothing, however, could stem the flow of refugees. It was steady, relentless, and unending. Thunderous artillery shook Saigon to its very foundations. The rolling wave of terror in rural areas pushed yet more refugees toward the capital. In other cities that had fallen, radio reports told of panic and anarchy in the streets. The refugees entering the city told frightening tales of carnage and death that came to those who could not escape. As I heard these reports, it only reinforced the obvious: the Saints must leave the country. It could be the difference between life and death. In any conceivable circumstance, if the city fell to the communists, those of us who had served in the conquered army and had associated with the Americans, even for religious reasons, would not be treated well. I was still saying *if* they came, even though they were right down the road. My mind still attempted to deny what I knew in my heart: defeat was at hand.

With President Wheat and Elder Bowman safely departed for Hong Kong, I returned to the business at hand. Two hundred and fifty Vietnamese Church members and their nonmember relatives were hoping and praying to be evacuated before Saigon fell. My job was to do all I could to make that happen. The rest was up to the Lord. I regarded the contacts I was given at the embassy through David Hoopes and President Wheat as our literal ticket to freedom. There were two high-priority groups we knew would be evacuated first. They were the American citizens still in Vietnam and the highly placed Vietnamese citizens who worked closely with the Americans in the embassy, the military, or the government. President Wheat had felt confident that members of the Church would be included in the next group of evacuees. I could only hope he was right.

I had one more major problem that required the Lord's intervention. I was needed continually at the branch to await word on the evacuation, but I was still in the army. I had applied for a discharge from the army sometime earlier based on my poor health, and I had not received an answer to my petition. My service in the army was thus in limbo. My four-year activation period had expired three years ago, and my size and weight remained below the official requirements. With the help of some high-ranking officers in the branch, I had submitted my petition to be released from the army. I had waited patiently for a ruling on my petition, but now I needed an answer fast. I did not know how I would be able to maintain contact twice a day with Mr. Currier while I was still on active duty with the Army of the Republic of Vietnam.

This problem weighed heavily on my mind, and I placed it before the Lord to solve. He did. Just when I needed to be available to interact with the embassy, my petition was partially granted. I was temporarily released from active duty with the right reserved to reevaluate my status at a later date. The effective date of my temporary release was not until May, but my commander kindly allowed me take leave until the new orders went into effect. Thus, I was suddenly available to devote my full attention to the planned evacuation of the members of the Saigon Branch, including my own family. I must acknowledge that the hand of the Lord manipulated the timing of these events for my benefit. I received permission to leave my post even as others were ordered to arms. It was a miracle.

There is a saying in the army: "Hurry up and wait." That saying describes my activities perfectly for the next few days. Life became a waiting game. I waited for news from the embassy. Branch members waited for news from me. The whole city waited for news from the defensive perimeter around Saigon. The more we waited, the more nervous we became. Even though I called the embassy twice per day as instructed, I never even spoke to my designated contact, Mr. Currier. Instead, his staff members always said the same thing: "Not yet. Not yet." This meant the evacuation program had not yet been implemented. I was given no message and no other instructions. The Saints, like most of Saigon, were going nowhere fast. Meanwhile, the war zone was drawing ever closer.

We tried to maintain our hope that somehow defeat could be averted, but despair and fear invaded our hearts. With each new day came more uncertainty and weariness of mind and spirit. Because I did not have a telephone at my house and needed to stay in contact with the embassy, and since the missionaries had vacated their quarters at the branch, I moved my family and myself to the branch building. There, I waited anxiously in my office for further word on our evacuation.

On April 21 our country's leader, President Thieu, resigned his office and fled Vietnam for the United States. This greatly upset the countrymen he left behind and dashed another measure of flickering hope in the hearts of the Saigon Saints. On the same day in Hong Kong, President Wheat advised the missionaries that they would not be returning to Vietnam and reassigned them to other areas within the mission. Nevertheless, he and others, including David Hoopes, worked furiously on our behalf. President Wheat was constantly contacting Church and government officials who were seeking information or who might be able to help. Brother Hoopes contacted Roger Shields of the U.S. Department of Defense. He in turn contacted Colonel John Madison in the Defense Attaché's Office in the U.S. embassy in Saigon. Colonel Madison was involved in searching for U.S. servicemen missing in action. Colonel Madison, independent of any efforts the embassy was making, was preparing to evacuate one hundred Vietnamese civilians who had worked for him and who would be marked for execution or imprisonment if Saigon fell. Colonel Madison told Shields he would do all he could to get the Saigon Saints on the many C-130 military flights leaving Saigon's Tan Son Nhut Air Base. I do not think these men were LDS, but their help was acquired through one Mormon the Lord definitely placed in the right place at the right time—David Hoopes.

On Tuesday, April 22, I was in the branch president's office in the chapel. I was reflecting upon the worsening predicament and my inability to get through to Mr. Currier. In that moment of great despair and disappointment, my phone rang. It was Colonel Madison. He told me that he was calling at the suggestion of David Hoopes and also mentioned President Wheat. Never has the feeling of impending doom so suddenly fled as when he explained to me his willingness and ability to help us in the evacuation. My joy was overwhelming as my heart swelled in thankfulness to the Lord for answering our fervent prayers. From that moment, I maintained close contact with Colonel Madison by telephone twice per day. I also attempted to reach Mr. Currier twice per day but had no contact with him.

On Thursday evening, April 24, I was again at the chapel maintaining my telephone vigil with my friend Colonel Kiem when the phone rang. I trembled in disbelief and excitement when Colonel Madison conveyed the message that we had been waiting so long to receive. It seemed too good to be true.

"Can you act fast, President Tay?" he asked.

"Yes, sir," I replied with confidence and anticipation. I thought he would tell me of a time in the next day or two.

"You have one hour, exactly, to gather twenty people to leave tonight."

I was astonished and speechless at the news. My momentary silence was broken by Colonel Madison's admonition that I hurry to an appointed place within the gates of Tan Son Nhut Airport and meet a Major Cook, who would await our arrival. I repeated back the instructions to be sure. Colonel Madison verified that my understanding was correct, and I hung up the phone.

I turned to Brother Kiem and said, "Gather your family. They are leaving here."

Our joy was full that the evacuation was beginning even as our hearts sank from the implications. I instructed Colonel Kiem as to where to be and what to bring. Kiem's family numbered eleven, leaving us with nine more seats to fill. I ran out of the office and asked my sister-in-law Le to ride her bicycle to some nearby homes and inform two other families of the opportunity to leave and the urgency involved. Quickly, the waiting game turned into a race against time. I drove at top speed to Tan Son Nhut Airport with another branch member, Major Ham.

We beheld a dreadful scene as we arrived at the airport. Thousands of people formed a sea of humanity surging at the airport gates. Razor-sharp barbed wire and threatening guns held them at bay. Airport security personnel were uneasy about the crowd, and I did not know if they would let us pass as we approached in a jeep dressed in our uniforms as officers of the South Vietnamese army. I prayed they would let us by, and they did. Soon, I located Colonel Madison, Major Cook, and Colonel Kiem. Colonel Kiem had brought his family as instructed, but there was no sign of the other families.

For Colonel Kiem and me, there was no thought of escape at that time. Brother Kiem felt that it would be impossible for him to leave because of his position with the armed forces of the Republic of Vietnam. I was very impressed that he asserted his authority only to save others. Colonel Kiem embraced his family one by one and gave them last-minute words of love and encouragement and hope for the future. We stood together and watched, our vision blurred by the tears in our eyes as his family boarded the waiting C-130 transport plane. We lingered a few moments until the aircraft had taxied away, rolled powerfully down the runway, lifted off the ground, and disappeared silently into the freedom of a billowing cloud.

We did not know whether to laugh or cry. We did both. But mainly we cried.

Colonel Kiem, Major Ham, and I struggled past the crowds and returned to the chapel. We found the two families there who had attempted to join Colonel Kiem's family on their flight to freedom. They had been prevented from entering the base and watched in total frustration as the aircraft left without them. They could not get into the airport because they did not have any papers from the U.S. embassy. Because Colonel Madison's help was independent of the embassy, there were no official papers. Some blamed me for their thwarted escape and believed that now they would never be able to escape. I began to feel a personal responsibility for the safety of those who had missed the plane. Perhaps, I thought, I could have done something differently. It was discouraging that the happy anticipation of a few hours before had changed into a feeling of miserable failure.

Early the next day, April 25, Colonel Madison called me with just what I needed: good news. He had arranged to reserve a few spaces on some departing C-130 aircraft. His arrangements, he said, were unofficial and through "the back door." That is, they were not related to the official evacuation plan of the embassy. I can testify that Colonel Madison's Department of Defense door was a lot more useful than the bureaucratic door of the State Department, which operated the embassy. Indeed, in view of the pitifully small degree of help being received through "official" embassy channels, how grateful I was for Colonel Madison and his "unofficial" help. That evening, a second group of ten members escaped Vietnam with the help of Colonel Madison.

On Saturday, April 26, I called all the branch members together for a meeting at the chapel. I advised them that anyone who could get inside the Tan Son Nhut Airport grounds should do so and remain inside the gates until they received further instructions. Those without means to get inside should at least remain camped nearby until we could find a way to get them inside. The only acceptable alternative to having proper papers was to be escorted by a high-ranking member of the military. All of the members of the branch told me that they were prepared to leave at a moment's notice.

By Sunday, April 27, about fifty branch members, including six or seven families, were at the airport. Could Heavenly Father gather fifty of his sheep from a throng of many thousands? Were our cries more urgent upon his ears than those of our brothers? Were our prayers more fervent than those of other families huddled together hoping for a miracle? We knew it was impossible to evacuate everyone waiting for a flight. We could not help but petition the Lord to make it possible for us to be among those that were evacuated. But it is a bittersweet prayer to ask to be saved with your family when perhaps the price might be that the man next to you and his family are left behind in the process.

Everyone in Saigon realized by now that time was running out. The war took a dramatic shift as Saigon came into the range of enemy rockets and mortar shells. The Viet Cong were at our very doors. It was said that our military was told to surrender or die. Indeed, last-minute negotiations being conducted concerned the terms of Saigon's surrender, not the cease-fire we prayed for. Rumors were rampant. Everyone could see that the Americans were being rapidly evacuated. Everyone could hear the sounds of war getting closer by the hour.

I served as president of the Saigon Branch, not by choice or ambition or ability. I only served because I was called to serve. When I was called, there were many higher authorities to help me. Now, with communication to the outside world virtually cut off, and with no missionaries or other Church leaders available, the leadership of the Saints had been thrust on me, the reluctant Saigon shepherd whose little flock was about to be scattered to the four winds. At times, in despair, I tried to humor myself. The Lord is surely here today, I reasoned. We were the only branch in the Church about to be invaded by communists. At other times, in my wavering, I asked myself if God cared what happened here. In the reaches of eternity, could He be concerned with the temporal fate of a few Vietnamese Saints? Was this one of those things He would allow to happen and work out later? Every explosion reminded us we might soon find out.

As difficult as that final sacrament meeting on April 27 was, the evacuation meeting that immediately followed was actually the most difficult meeting of my life.

In the evacuation meeting, there were many problems to discuss. I was now free to tell the Saints the whole story about how the evacuation list was made and placed with the embassy. I explained that the evacuations that had already taken place were not done through the official evacuation plan but by special help provided through a Church member close to the president of the United States. I then revealed the actual plan. The main concern with it was that only family members who were Church members or investigators were on the list of about three hundred persons. If the government evacuation was limited to just those on the list, some other family members would be left behind. Some members who belonged to part-member families asked, "What about my family who are not members of the Church?" They would cry in pain, "I cannot leave without my family!" The anguish and sorrow they expressed was my own. While I genuinely understood their concern, fear, and grief, I could not bear being blamed personally for the potential separations and loss of loved ones they might experience if the evacuation plan was implemented. I decided to make this a matter for the priesthood to work out. I asked the heads of each family group to meet together privately to make some very difficult decisions. Feeling that our time was running short, it became necessary to decide which of the members would be evacuated first. This was a heartrending decision that I did not want to make alone. Those present at the meeting decided that the first to leave should be those who had been members of the Church the longest and those who held Church positions. It was decided that my own family should be evacuated first. I thanked them for that kindness, and then I volunteered to be the last one to board the evacuation aircraft. This would leave me free to help the other members without having to concern myself with my family while I shuttled between the airport and the chapel. I felt that my responsibility as branch president and as the Lord's appointed servant in Vietnam left me no alternative.

The plan was approved by the heads of families and an order of departure was agreed upon. Now, when Colonel Madison called, I would know who was next, and they would know also. We actually assumed that all would be evacuated, so the particular order was more of an organizational matter than a matter of life and death. As last man on the list, I especially hoped that was the case.

Those fifty to sixty branch members on the airport grounds could not attend the meetings on Sunday, so I drove there to report to them what took place. They seemed pleased with the decisions made and joined in the hope that all who desired to leave could do so. Meanwhile, after the evacuation meeting, in accordance to the agreement, my wife and family were driven to the airport to await their opportunity to leave Vietnam. I met them there and my heart broke as the reality of our impending separation set in. I told my dear wife that I had to stay in Vietnam awhile longer and that we might next meet in heaven because I did not know if I would ever get out of Vietnam. I told her I loved her and would be thinking of her. If something should prevent our reunion, I asked her to raise the boys in the Church so they could receive the priesthood.

While at the airport, I called Colonel Madison on the military phone line, since the civilian phones were an impossible mess to get through. His tone of voice was one of extreme urgency as he told of his efforts to forestall disaster. He told me that he had acted as the leader of a negotiating team that had just returned from a meeting with the North Vietnamese. A promise was obtained from the communist forces that there would be no blood bath in Saigon, as was generally feared when the communist forces succeeded in their campaign. Somehow, Colonel Madison's assurances were not very comforting. Fear began to penetrate my soul. Colonel Madison tried to comfort me, but I could not be comforted. He tried to convince me that there was no reason to be worried. I replied that he did not realize the responsibilities that I bore to look after the members of the branch. He was unaware of the times I had looked into the faces of the members to see expressions of hope riding so precariously over the surface of confusion and fear. I could not take the hope away. I told the colonel that I was accountable for my people and that now I feared for their lives.

Colonel Madison suggested that I send my family out on the next plane. Since I already had the support of the branch to do this, I agreed to his suggestion. I told him if he could get the seats, I would have my family ready. I hung up the phone and returned to the adjacent room where the members of the branch at the airport were waiting restlessly for word. I told them of my conversation with Colonel Madison and told them to remain on the airport grounds if they wanted to be evacuated. Somehow, in this reserve of peace amid the confusion that reigned all about us, I had a renewed glimmer of hope that we could all be evacuated before Saigon was overrun. I kept assuring myself silently that there would be enough time. I felt consumed by the solitary goal of saving the branch members from the invading communists. While we were living moment by moment, waiting for danger to pass, I could not permit myself any further thoughts of failure. Everyone was depending on me.

I left the airport Sunday evening to return to the branch chapel, where President Wheat had made an appointment to call at 8:00 P.M. Just as I arrived at the chapel, the phone rang; I answered it, expecting to hear President Wheat. Instead, I was told that just after I had left the airport, Colonel Madison provided my family space on an outgoing flight to Guam. They were gone. I had expected one more good-bye. One more farewell embrace. But suddenly and swiftly they were gone. My wife and our three children and my wife's mother and sisters were off to an unknown fate in a faraway land. I felt that all would be well and that we would be reunited, but how could we know?

President Wheat did not call and could not call. I decided to send a telegram: "PLEASE COME TO SAIGON IMMEDIATELY. HELP SOLVE DIFFICULTIES HERE. CAN RETURN SAME DAY." I did not know if it was impossible for President Wheat to return to Saigon. I didn't even know if he could help. I only knew I needed help. I thought an American might have better luck than I was having dealing with Mr. Currier at the embassy. President Wheat had been forceful and effective in dealing with the embassy on his last visit. I felt like I needed to be in two places at once: the branch office and the airport. President Wheat would know what to do, I thought.

Several members of the branch volunteered to remain at the chapel to await news of further evacuation. On Monday, April 28, Colonel Madison called me and informed me, to the delight of the people on the list, that another ten seats would be available Monday evening. Our spirits were raised by the news, and we began to hope for a complete evacuation again. But later in the day, he phoned again to tell us the seats would not be available after all. Someone with higher priority would be using them. The members who were scheduled to leave were deeply saddened but nonetheless continued to have faith that their turn would come. I was not so sure anymore.

Throughout the day on Monday, mass confusion enveloped the capital. People wanted to run, but where? People wanted to take money out of banks and buy food, provisions, and fuel for their motorbikes. Everyone wanted everything, and they all wanted it at once. I found it difficult to remain calm in the presence of such hysteria. The communists were in sight of the city. Many said they could take the city at will. Perhaps they were waiting for the evacuation to be completed, I thought wishfully. Late Monday evening, they shelled the airport run-way and damaged it badly. I couldn't have wished more vainly.

Tuesday morning, April 29, I was still at the chapel, hoping for another call from someone, anyone, with good news. I found out later what had happened at the airport. With ten thousand Vietnamese civilians waiting inside the airport at the immigrant staging area and on the runway, plus thousands more outside the gates, panic was setting in. Two C-130s, maintaining contact with the White House, circled overhead waiting for instructions. Finally, they dropped down to attempt a landing, but they found it impossible because the runway was damaged from shelling, littered with debris, and swarming with people. Those two C-130s and others that had been dispatched from the Philippines were ordered to return to their bases.

When the aircraft turned away without landing, the crowds began to despair and some began to riot. The people were out of control. They covered the runways and beat on the buildings; outside, they clawed and pulled at the fences. Our little group of branch members tried to stay together but found it difficult to do with so much movement in the crowd. Everyone was emotionally crushed by the assumed termination of the evacuation. Some people left the airport and sought some other way out of the city, but most people just vented their anger and frustration on one another. With the runway shelled relentlessly, Tan Son Nhut Airport was officially declared closed.

A few long hours after the C-130s turned away, on the afternoon of April 29, a new sound was heard in the sky. It was the sound of Operation Frequent Wind. It was the sound of helicopters. Back in Washington, President Ford had made a decision to go ahead with Operation Frequent Wind and had ordered into action scores of helicopters and thousands of Marines poised on ships in the South China Sea. President Ford wanted every American out immediately. Only a fraction of the thousands of Vietnamese waiting could be taken out now. Still, tears flowed freely among the branch members and everyone at the airport when three huge dual-rotor American helicopters dropped out of the clouds and prepared to land. U.S. Marines poured out of the helicopters as they touched down and formed a protective line to secure a landing area. Dozens of other helicopters came into view. Once they landed, people were hurriedly filed on and shuttled off on a forty-five-minute flight to waiting ships off the coast of Vietnam. There they were quickly unloaded so the helicopters could return. The process was repeated over and over again. Through it all, I was confined to the chapel because the government had declared a twenty-four-hour curfew. The Americans in Saigon were being extracted from the embassy and other designated areas as quickly as possible. They were ordered out of Vietnam within twenty-four hours. We interpreted this as a last desperate effort to appease the North Vietnamese. I assumed that it referred only to military personnel and continued to place calls to the embassy, always to no avail.

When I learned the airport was closed, I became extremely distressed. Until then, I had been able to mentally separate the Vietnamese Saints from the thousands of my countrymen who were also seeking to escape. I felt, because of our faith and all that was being done by others outside of Vietnam, by Church leaders in Salt Lake City, and by well-placed U.S. government officials, that members of the branch would be spared capture by our enemies. For an installation so valuable as the Tan Son Nhut Airport to be closed signaled a fatal blow to the war effort.

I contacted Colonel Madison as soon as possible, and he informed me that the C-130 flights had been suspended due to heavy damage on the runway. Helicopters were being used to evacuate Vietnamese and Americans at the airport and at the embassy, but the colonel was not able to be of any further help with seating. The evacuation plan we had relied on for our deliverance was no longer in force. His words seemed unreal. Not able to help any further? My entire hope rested with him, and now he could not help. The helicopters were not taking reservations; they landed, filled up like so many seagulls gulping up crickets, then flew off to regurgitate them on waiting ships and returned for more. In my shock and despair, I could only manage a subdued thank-you for his previous help and bade Colonel Madison a sad good-bye. He had done his best; of that I was certain. In fact, I recalled that not a single branch member was ever evacuated under the official evacuation plan. It was only through the efforts of Colonel Madison, who befriended us at the behest of Brother Hoopes, that any Saigon Saint secured passage on a C-130 aircraft. I then reasoned that maybe the helicopters, with no reservation required, would provide a better chance of evacuation to those already at the airport than had the C-130s. That is what I hoped, and that is how it was.

Colonel Doan Viet Lieu's daughter, Thu Anh, kept a record of her experience during the helicopter evacuation. As it is one shared by most of the Saints who escaped in that manner, I will relate it here. Thu Anh's father, Colonel Lieu, had been introduced to the gospel five months before by his nephew. The entire Doan family had joined the Church in March, just before the missionaries were evacuated. Colonel Lieu was visiting his family at the airport when the shelling that closed the runway occurred. A curfew imposed after the shelling prevented his leaving, and he abandoned the idea of returning to his doomed military post. He finally considered the advice of his friends and family to leave with them. He discarded his military uniform, donned his son's pajamas, and prepared to leave Vietnam with his family and nothing more.

Thu Anh and her family huddled together through the shelling along with the others massed inside the airport gates. When the shelling prevented the airplanes from using the runways, the people were filled with hopelessness. Some left the airport and joined the throngs that filled the highways leading away from the city. Among those who remained, the fear increased tenfold. Fear changed to hope when the helicopters arrived and resumed the evacuation. Flanked by marines, Thu Anh and her family waited in the long lines for their turn. Finally, on a signal from the soldiers, Thu Anh and her sister, each carrying a little brother, ran up the lowered ramp into a waiting helicopter. Suddenly, the ramp was raised and the helicopter took off. Thu Anh was panicked to see that not all her family was on board. Her parents and several others were missing. She looked around anxiously and, besides her sister and two brothers, could find only her grandmother. My wife's little brother, Liem, was also aboard this helicopter.

Their particular helicopter deposited its cargo forty-five minutes later on the USS *Duluth,* one of the U.S. warships waiting just off the Vietnam coast. Once unloaded, they immediately went back for more people. The procedure continued nonstop for several hours until communist advances made it unsafe for even the helicopters to fly. The marines who came on the first helicopters were the last ones to leave. Suddenly, the airlift was over. Everyone else would have to find another way out.

Thu Anh and her companions were transferred to another ship late that night and were dumbfounded when they found the ship already crammed from stem to stern with fleeing refugees. In conditions of extreme crowding and insufficient food, they sailed for Guam, a ten-day trip. The time passed slowly. They were extremely distressed because they did not know the fate of their parents and the rest of their brothers and sisters. Weary and hungry, on Sunday, May 4, they observed fast Sunday and felt somewhat comforted. Finally, on May 7, the group arrived in Guam. After several hours of paperwork, they were taken by bus to the refugee center. The first thing Thu Anh saw when the bus stopped was her father! He was serving as an interpreter and was meeting every bus, looking for his children. They all burst into tears of joy upon seeing one another and thanked God the family was together again.

I spent the night of April 29 in my office at the chapel, where I prayed for new ways of escape. I refused to accept the notion that there was no way to help the remainder of the branch. Surely we would not be abandoned. I used the telephone to call the U.S. embassy. No one answered. Because of the curfew in effect and our location next to the police station, I dared not sneak out during curfew. I spent another night in the chapel trying continually to contact the embassy.

On April 30, I felt I must go to the embassy to see Mr. Currier myself. Perhaps he could call David Hoopes again. Surely something could be done for us. Lieutenant Colonel Loi, a branch member, came to the chapel with his jeep, and we drove toward the embassy. Along the route, thousands of people were ransacking various American buildings. The looting stunned me, and I worried what I might find at the embassy.

When we drew close to the embassy, smoke was rising from the structure, which was partly in flames. Crowds had gathered outside, and many articles of furniture and office equipment lay scattered about in an attempt to save it from the fire. Saigon Fire Department personnel worked frantically to put out the flames. The embassy was vacant. I could not believe that the Americans had deserted the embassy. The shock was indescribable. I felt like I was falling off a tall building. I felt an empty hopelessness that caused me to weep openly. What was I to do? How could I face the remaining members of the branch whom I had promised safe conduct out of Vietnam? How would I ever see my beautiful wife and children again?

Brother Loi and I returned to the chapel. Several of the branch members were there. We learned that possibly as many as one hundred branch members had escaped in the helicopters or C-130s, while perhaps 150 of us were left behind. (Actual estimates using the official evacuation list and comparing it to the names of those who made it to Guam or other staging sites indicate that 186 were presumed to be evacuated and 203 were presumed not to be evacuated. These numbers include Church members and their nonmember relatives.) We were devastated that the evacuation plan was not more successful.

Dr. Nghia suggested going to the International Red Cross to seek help in evacuating the others by boat or some other means. Lacking any other plan, we ventured an attempt. I rode with Dr. Nghia on his Honda motorbike. We were traveling along a one-way street when people came running from the opposite direction. They were shouting and crying, "The communists are coming!" Then we saw a big tank coming down the road toward us. We had never seen a big Russian tank before. It had a huge gun and big, wide tracks. Dr. Nghia veered the Honda off the road. We fell off the Honda and tried to hide in a ditch. The tank went by very close. The ground shook like an earthquake. It was terrible. All of the people running past us were very frightened. When the tank passed, we got back onto the Honda and went back to the branch. We could hear guns firing all around us. About twenty of the Saigon Saints stayed inside the chapel because we dared not leave. We cried for ourselves and for our people. We looked at one another in disbelief over our perilous and seemingly hopeless situation. We thought of those who had escaped whom we might never see again and of those of us left behind to face a conquering army. What an incredible day! It was April 30, 1975. Saigon had fallen. The life we knew was over, and a life we never cared to know was just beginning.

CHAPTER 8

And Great Was the Fall Thereof

On April 30, immediately after the American evacuation was completed, the Saigon government surrendered unconditionally to the North Vietnamese. Saigon had fallen, and great was the fall thereof. South Vietnamese military personnel removed their boots and uniforms and littered the streets with all vestiges of their former associations and attempted to blend in with the civilian masses. Vietnamese civilians, angry over the American departure and the government's defeat, began to riot and loot throughout Saigon in an insane effort to strike back at those who had left them in this perilous condition. They broke into many businesses and hauled off their inventory of appliances, tools, building materials, and anything else they could carry. They broke windows and started fires and picked fights with one another over who was at fault for the loss of the war. Meanwhile, our president and many of the high-ranking South Vietnamese officials, whose personal corruption is widely blamed for the government's collapse, had already been safely evacuated to freedom, usually with their gold and other valuables in their possession. The high frustration level among the average citizens, helpless to help themselves, could not be measured or contained.

Their frustration was not limited to Vietnamese leaders who had fled the country. A good share of the pent-up anger so freely flowing in the streets during the aftermath of our unconditional surrender was directed at the Americans. Such feelings are not hard to understand. Over the years of American involvement in the war, American Presidents Kennedy ("We'll pay any price and bear any burden"), Johnson ("America will never desert you"), and Nixon ("We will bring peace with honor") repeatedly promised that America would never permit the communists to prevail in our struggle for liberty. In 1973 the Americans withdrew, and two years later we lost the battle to preserve our freedom. This sad reality does not diminish in any way the sacrifice of those Americans who died trying to save us from a communist takeover. The Savior's teaching applies to those Americans killed in our war to the same extent as those killed defending freedom anywhere: "Greater love hath no man than this, that a man lay down his life for his friends" (John 15:13). No, South Vietnam's fall does not diminish the great sacrifice of those who died trying to secure our freedom. It does not negate the service of anyone who was sent to Vietnam and returned home with wounds, either physical or psychological, from his service. They did their best. It was not their fault that we lost the war. I will always believe that their cause was just. Our freedom was no less worthy of defending than that of a Filipino or a Frenchman in World War II, or, later on, that of a Korean, a Kuwaiti, or an Iraqi. History shows that after the Tet Offensive, the price of our freedom was simply deemed too high to pay after all. It was a political decision, and not a military one, to accept defeat. For those of us who were among the defeated, understanding why we were ultimately abandoned did not make defeat any more palatable.

The Saigon Branch was just another casualty of the war. We were left to ourselves with our enemies at our very gates, salivating and pacing like packs of hungry wolves. For myself, Cao Minh, Sister Vy, Dr. Nghia, Le Van Kha, and all those Saints who gathered together in the chapel because we did not know where else to go, there was also anger, but mainly despair and dreadful apprehension about what might happen next. With the Americans gone, the missionaries gone, the helicopters gone, the mighty U.S. embassy in flames, and communist troops streaming into the city, our options seemed few and our situation hopeless. While thus huddled together inside the chapel, we heard the angry shouts of mobs in the neighborhood. They were dismantling and looting all of the American homes in the area where the chapel was located. Suddenly, the gate leading from the street to the chapel burst open, and a mob surged forward in anticipation of finding more treasures.

We could not allow the mob to destroy the Lord's chapel. Brother Cao Minh and I, along with a few young men from the branch, met the crowd at the entrance. For a few moments, we stood face-to-face, defying the invading throng while earnestly praying within ourselves that there would be no serious confrontation. In buildings surrounding us, they had taken everything of value, including the glass from the windows, sinks off the walls, and toilets off the floor. The other structures around us had been stripped clean, and now they felt it was our turn.

With the strength of servants of the Lord, we boldly told them this was not a home but a church that contained nothing left by the Americans. We told them it was part of the Chinese school, which we had rented for our meetings. For several minutes, the menacing crowd inched closer and threatened us with harm if we did not move out of their way. We assured them that we could not allow them to desecrate our church and pleaded with them to leave us in peace. Our combined silent prayers for deliverance from this mob were offered secretly in our hearts and rewarded openly. At last, the mob succumbed to a power greater than ours, as we believe God moved upon them to leave. They quieted and turned away in reluctant retreat. They continued their pillaging further down the street.

On the other side of the city, communist soldiers marched triumphantly behind a parade of Russian-made tanks and captured American jeeps. Shots could be heard as small pockets of resistance were extinguished. Surprisingly, the Viet Cong and North Vietnamese Army were under orders not to harm any of the population, just as Colonel Madison had said. For the most part, the orders were observed. Many of the conquerors were nothing more than barefoot teenagers in black pajamas, members of the Viet Cong. The rest were uniformed soldiers from the regular army of North Vietnam. On blaring loudspeakers, they declared themselves to be friends of the people, who only wished to end the war and reunite the country. Although selective bullets continued to fly against those who resisted, the communists tried to appear reasonable. They said the curfews and restrictions of freedoms they imposed were only temporary and necessary to restore proper order. All of this was designed to calm the citizens and get their cooperation in the change of government from a free society to a communist regime. Looting in the city abruptly ceased when the new government promised to shoot and kill any offenders. Many of the captured guns of police, militia, civilian, and military personnel were confiscated and brought to the police station next to the chapel. The road outside the chapel was soon piled high with stacks of guns and implements of war.

For two days, varying numbers of branch members stayed inside the chapel as much as possible to avoid the uncertain and potentially dangerous situations around us. Wandering bands of thugs and armed Northern forces spread out into every neighborhood of the city. Branch members left behind after the airlift cautiously made their way back to the chapel to seek counsel or to complain or both. Some were very distraught and angry with me for not doing more or beginning the evacuation sooner. These things were not in my control, of course, and most calmed down when they realized that I had done my best and that, furthermore, I was in the same predicament they were. We counseled one with another and shared what knowledge we had and also what rumors we had heard about current conditions in the city. We discussed our limited options in view of the new situation in our homeland. Because some people had definitely been killed or severely punished for their American connections, we feared for our lives. After several more hours, most members went back to their homes. Six of us remained in the chapel, still concerned for our lives if we left. The six included myself, Cao Minh, Dr. Nghia, Brother Nghia, and two of the young men who had faced down the mob. We foolishly hoped the nonfunctioning telephone would somehow ring and President Wheat or Colonel Madison or someone, anyone, would call and tell us what we should do. No one called.

Over the course of our two days of waiting, we six gradually determined that we might as well attempt an escape from Vietnam as fall into the hands of our captors, where our military and religious connections would be revealed sooner or later.

In my own case, I had the double incentive of being reunited with my beloved Lien and our three precious children. Already I missed them so greatly that I trembled. I could not bear the thought of living out my life in Vietnam without ever looking upon them or caressing their sweet souls again. For myself, Brother Minh, and several others, the way seemed clear. We must leave Vietnam.

Brother Nghia had a brother who was a communist in an area about two hundred miles southwest of Saigon. He suggested we go there and escape, if not from the country, at least to a place where one of those in authority, his brother, might provide us refuge. None of us having a better idea, we decided to go to Cape Ca Mau, the southernmost point in South Vietnam.

In the predawn hours of Friday, May 2, we slipped out of the chapel and walked to a bus stop where we boarded a big passenger bus headed west for the Mekong Delta. The bus, with seating for about fifty, was soon overcrowded. Every seat was filled, and all of the standing room was taken. A dozen or more people hung out of the back emergency door of the bus, and the worldly goods of many passengers were piled high on the roof. There were so many refugees entering Saigon from the countryside that the North Vietnamese did not seem to care if a busload of hapless Vietnamese departed. Travel was very slow and hazardous. Five times our bus was stopped by Viet Cong or North Vietnamese regular army soldiers, who, acting on their own, searched the bus looking for gold or valuables to steal, or foreigners to detain or kill. We proceeded from city to city, always subject to harassment as the bus stopped to offload some passengers and board others. When we reached the Mekong River, Vietnam's Mississippi, we had to cross on a rickety ferry boat and wondered if the ferry bearing our burgeoning bus would make it across the mighty

Mekong, but somehow it did. There were many North Vietnamese soldiers visible lining both sides of the river. Boats full of Vietnamese citizens trying to flee the country had to pass by these soldiers before they could take the river to the sea and on to Thailand. North Vietnamese gunboats also patrolled the river and the offshore waters where the Mekong flowed into the ocean. After our ferry crossing, we pressed on southward toward the Cape of Vietnam and Cape Ca Mau. Our desired goal was to somehow reach Thailand, and to do this, we must first reach the sea. When the helicopters stopped flying a few days before, many citizens had turned to the sea as their next best hope for escape. Rumors through the crowds of refugees flooding out of the city told us of foreign ships waiting just outside territorial waters to pick up those who could avoid swarms of communist gunboats along the way. (In fact, Brother George Reading from the Saigon Branch was in charge of one such ship. He was directly responsible for saving hundreds of fleeing Vietnamese.) If you did not make it past the gunboats, at least your death would be swift.

After two days on the bus, our weary group of six Saigon Saints arrived at the Cape of Vietnam. The sight of the ocean's unobstructed expanse somehow gave us hope that we would finally escape. I began to believe that soon I would be with my family again and that the nightmare for myself and those who accompanied me would be over. I couldn't help worrying for the many Latter-day Saints still in Vietnam. I prayed unceasingly that all of the members of the branch would be preserved by the Lord's hand.

We worked our way down to the shoreline and found to our horror that the formerly bustling fishing villages and docks were totally without boats. None were available anywhere. Just days earlier, remnants of the retreating South Vietnamese Army had commandeered anything that floated and had fled the country. Although we located some damaged craft that were partially submerged, our chances of finding a usable boat were one in a million. Scuttled boats could be of no help to us.

We continued south to Cape Ca Mau in search of an escape route. Ca Mau lies at the most extreme southern point in Vietnam, about two hundred miles from Saigon. It was there that our party separated by day to explore possible avenues and means of escape and met together again each night. We discussed our observations and inquiries of the day and reasoned together as to how we could escape the communists. All the while we slept at the home of a communist, Brother Nghia's brother, who lived in a nearby village. This was an uneasy association for the rest of us, but we trusted in Brother Nghia's assurances that we were safe there. His assessment proved accurate, and we settled into a routine. Each day, we went our separate ways to seek a possible path to freedom, which we hoped to share with the others when we reunited in the evening.

For my part, every day at first light, I went to the ocean's edge and climbed over a pile of rocks that jutted out into the sea. I took my position on an elevated rock, which provided an unobstructed view of the ocean. I hoped to sight a friendly ship and signal it by reflecting mirror or signal fire. This plan was naive and not worthy of hope, but my prior experiences in desperate circumstances gave me faith that a miracle could happen. Day after day, I sat on my lookout rock and anxiously scanned the horizon for ships and prayed for another miracle. I became lost in my thoughts of my family and my precious wife. I wondered what she was doing and where she was and whether she was being cared for adequately. I wondered if she wondered where I was right at that moment, but I knew she could not imagine my being on a lookout rock so far from our Saigon home. I thought of God and His plan for me. I thought of the branch members and my responsibilities for them. For over a week, I sat on my rock and thought and looked and prayed, becoming nearly hypnotized by the vastness and deep blue emptiness of the ocean's surface before me.

I did not see a single vessel the entire time I sat on my rock. Very reluctantly, I finally became convinced that it was pointless to remain. On the evening of the tenth day, with saddened eyes, I watched the sun as it sank into the sea, leaving behind a painted sky of brilliant shades of orange and red. My vigil at Cape Ca Mau was over. I was a captive in my own land.

I advised my companions that evening that our answer did not lie in this remote outpost and that we would have to return to Saigon. It had occurred to us that perhaps we would not be allowed to go back to the capital because of the new restrictions being installed by the communist government. Everything we had was in Saigon; if we could not leave Vietnam, we had to go back.

We had come to Ca Mau before the government organized its bureaucracy based on permits and proper papers. Going back would be difficult without the government's blessing, but we didn't know how that could be obtained. The answer came through Brother Nghia's brother, who was a captain in the communist forces. During our visit, he became sympathetic to our plight. Being wise to the ways of the new government, he helped us develop a scheme that might convince the authorities to let us return to Saigon. Although we were not accustomed to being devious and investing in lies, in the face of overwhelming odds and with no other weapons at our disposal, we determined that, in order to survive, at times we would have to use cunning and deception. We told the local officials about the sunken boats we had discovered and suggested that they could be raised and repaired. "Should they not be put into use to help provide food for the village, rather than sit in the ocean?" we reasoned. "If we had the parts and the tools, we could repair the boats. If we could go to Saigon, we could get the tools we needed." Such was our case. The local authorities weighed the benefits such a salvage effort would bring and finally consented to grant us permission to go to Saigon for the parts and tools, but they would only allow me to leave. I could not leave my friends. I prevailed upon the communists to send us all, as all would be needed in a project of this size and all had different but necessary skills in the marketplace, whereas no man by himself knew as much as the whole group. Once again, the authorities considered the proposal and gave their permission. They issued the proper papers for all of us to go to Saigon and back. Once again, the Lord's spirit overcame the opposition and stubbornness of our oppressors.

Although we had fabricated our intentions, the plan was even beginning to sound good to us. Perhaps if we could fix a boat, we could also take it on its maiden voyage—straight to Thailand. But for the time being, it looked like we would have to face the music, whatever that entailed, in Saigon.

We left for Saigon as we had come. Our bus ride back was not so crowded as before, because it was stopped at every town and passengers were checked for proper papers. No papers, no bus ride. Everyone had a photo identification card from the previous government, but that was not enough. Papers or official letters of permission from the new government that explained the purpose of your travels were required. Properly papered, we retraced our route and two days later arrived at Saigon.

While we were away, the communists had changed the name of Saigon to Ho Chi Minh City, to honor their late leader who had driven the French out of Vietnam in 1954 and had spent the rest of his life leading the effort to conquer South Vietnam. It will always be Saigon to those of us who remember the city in her glory. Strikingly modern and advanced by the North's standards, Saigon is beautifully situated near both the bounteous South China Sea fisheries and the rich rice and agricultural areas of the Mekong Delta. The North had nothing to compare with Saigon.

When our group of six arrived in Saigon, some members immediately informed me that the communists had taken over the building we used as our chapel. The curators of the Chinese school where our branch building was located had fled the country, leaving the entire complex to be confiscated. The Church materials and furniture we had saved from the ransacking mobs were about to be stripped from us again. We had to act fast to save them.

I asked Sister Vy, Cao Minh, and Dr. Nghia to gather up the branch members they could find and come to the branch president's office to discuss what to do about the situation. My sadness increased tenfold when I learned that some of the members remained angry with me because they had not been evacuated. Some still blamed me personally for the evacuation plan's failure. Some also complained of my recent attempt to escape without them. Such comments left me heartbroken, because I truly was concerned with each member's well-being. I had done my best to help them leave, but the evacuation was over. What was I to do? It was not possible for me to orchestrate a new evacuation. The sad fact was that we had missed our opportunity to leave as a group. I counseled anyone who could find a way to leave with his or her family on their own to do so. In the meantime, I felt compelled to continue in whatever way I could to try to keep our people together. However good my intentions were, the desperation of the situation and the growing discord among the members forced me to make another difficult decision. We had to give up our claim to our chapel. The communists, already occupying the chapel, clearly would not relinquish the building to us. Our best hope was to salvage its contents before we were obliged to leave empty-handed. We agreed as a group to voluntarily relinquish the building, which we did not own anyway and only rented, in exchange for the right to remove those items that belonged to us. The communists agreed, although there was nothing we could have done if they had chosen not to agree.

Sister Vy offered the home of a relative who had departed Vietnam as a storage place for the furniture and materials we could haul away. Church-printed materials had previously been destroyed to prevent any possible actions against the members. We had no means to haul the branch property away and were forced to sell the piano and one of the desks so that we could get money to rent a truck. Money left over was used as a fast-offering fund to help needy families in the branch.

Many suspicious eyes watched as we removed the last of the Church's furniture and property and carefully placed it in the truck. At any moment, the crowds could decide that we were somehow a deserving target and lash out at us. Fortunately, we were spared from such an attack, although the fear lingered with us until our task was completed.

We attempted to hold a regular sacrament service in Sister Vy's relative's home, but the communists questioned why we came together in such a group. They restricted any gatherings of more than three persons and required that a report be made anytime a meeting took place. With our chapel confiscated, our membership scattered and fragmented, and our new government restricting our ability to meet with one another, the Saigon Branch, for all intents and purposes, ceased to exist, except in our hearts.

The extent of our scattering was not known to me at the time nor was the extent of the love and assistance being given those who had been evacuated. Most of the evacuated Saigon Saints, including my wife and children, were at that time in Guam at a hastily assembled refugee camp set up at Anderson Air Force Base. Elders Dee Oviatt and Richard Bowman were sent to Guam by President Wheat to search for Saigon Saints among the masses of evacuated Vietnamese and provide them with all assistance possible. The missionaries remained there until June 5, 1975, by which time all of the evacuated Saints had been safely relocated in the United States. At least five refugee camps were set up, including the largest one at Camp Pendleton, California, where my wife and family arrived. They came just one day after President Spencer W. Kimball visited the Church members in the camp. He inquired after my wife's whereabouts and, learning that she had not yet arrived, left her a personal message with one of the presiding elders. He instructed him to seek her out and deliver the message as soon as possible. The message was: "I testify that your husband will be preserved and that you will be reunited as a family in the Lord's own due time." He added that he hoped the time would be soon.

Elder Bowman's mission ended while he was still in Guam, and he returned home. Elder Oviatt and Elder Elmer were reassigned to Fort Chaffee, Arkansas, where another of the refugee camps was established. Camps were also established at Elgin Air Force Base, Florida; Indian Gap, Indiana; and Pennsylvania. Missionaries assigned to these camps, some formerly in Saigon, not only sought out Saigon Saints but also, using the pamphlets translated by the translation committee and preserved by the departing missionaries, began to teach the gospel to some of the humble Vietnamese refugees.

The entire Church held a special fast for all the Vietnamese "boat people" and the evacuated Saigon Saints shortly after President Kimball's visit to Camp Pendleton. The Church provided much relief and supplies to those suddenly homeless souls, now without a country and without any worldly possessions. Almost all of the evacuated Saigon Saints were provided with sponsors by the Church and went to live where their sponsors were. Most of them stayed in California. My wife and family went to Provo, Utah. As I said, I knew nothing of these events at the time. My problems were closer at hand, with those still in Saigon.

After getting our property from the branch, my thoughts turned to Cao Minh and others of us who were in jeopardy. We concocted another plan. Partly to prove to the communists that we Saints were not subversives, I provided the local chief with an itemized list of everything we had "voluntarily" turned over to them at our chapel. The list even contained luxury items such as an air conditioning unit. At the same time, I requested that Brother Cao Minh, who had long been an officer in the South Vietnamese Air Force, be permitted to come live with me. I fabricated a story about Brother Cao Minh living in the chapel and now being without a home. It was very dangerous for Cao Minh because of his former military status, which we thought would surely bring reprisals to him. Once we had obtained permission for him to live with me, we invented another story about him being a draft dodger, a valuable person in the eyes of the communists. Had they learned the truth, we would have been severely punished.

Cao Minh, Dr. Nghia, and I continued to plan how we might escape. The other Brother Nghia decided to go back to

SAIGON BRANCH REFUGEES AT USMC CAMP PENDLETON, CALIFORNIA, MAY 1975
(photograph courtesy Ruth C. Kovalenko and Al Ostraff)

live temporarily with his communist brother in Ca Mau. Later, he moved back to Saigon and married a young woman from the branch. The other two young men from our group went their separate ways. Money was an absolute necessity for any escape attempt to have a possibility of success. Dr. Nghia had enough money to finance our escape by paying our passage on a boat leaving Vietnam, but we still needed to make the necessary contacts. In the meantime, we decided that we three would strive to be cooperative and inconspicuous.

The communists soon issued an edict that all those citizens who had served in the South Vietnamese armed forces were required to report to the authorities for a brief "reeducation" program. Cao Minh was afraid not to report for fear of being discovered and punished. I reminded him that I had testified on his behalf that he was a draft dodger. If he should report to the authorities that he was an officer, my testimony would be refuted and it could cause me great problems. I advised him that he should report as a draft dodger and not list any relatives. We agreed that his story should also include that he was the only son of a family that lived in a western area. This would protect his sisters in Saigon from any threat of harm.

Our fabrications were devised to frustrate the cunning plans of the enemy. The whole circumstance of the call to report for reeducation seemed very suspicious to me. I sensed there was a lingering desire for revenge that had not yet manifested itself, and I feared that we were going to be punished. The communists knew that unless they tricked us, they would not be able to tell the officers from the enlisted men. It seemed important to them that an example be made of those who had fought against them, and yet nearly the entire male population of the Republic of South Vietnam had at one time been involved in the military. They needed the former military people to grow the food and rebuild the country; they could not send everyone to prison.

It was announced afterward by loudspeakers that reeducation was to be done by rank. In the first call to report, the draftees and enlisted soldiers were summoned. Officers from second lieutenant to general did not have to report at that time. Those who were not officers numbered in the millions. The general instruction was that reeducation would require only three days. At the conclusion, the participants would be returned home with certificates in hand commemorating the successful completion of their reeducation. This is precisely what happened.

After the first group had returned safely in just three days, a second call was issued for the officers and officials who had held positions in government and industry. Those who ranked from second lieutenant to captain were instructed to bring a ten-day supply of food; those from major to general were to bring a thirty-day supply. We assumed that our reeducation would take a little longer than that of our enlisted brothers, because, in the eyes of the communists, we had been more sinful than they had.

When the order for officers to report was issued, Dr. Nghia and I didn't bother to report at first. We thought that perhaps if we did not report and instead remained home, we might be overlooked. This would give us time to plan our escape. Some who had previously sought to escape even changed their minds temporarily. They reasoned that perhaps the new government should be given a chance. The government constantly reassured us that our desire to return to a normal peacetime life would be honored except for a few rules of necessity. We were told that a master plan would soon be introduced that would free us from the enslavement brought to our country by the capitalists. They said the new society would be equal, where the rich could no longer oppress the poor. A number of radical changes came to our city as waves of new edicts were issued "for our own good."

One of the first massive changes was announced at midnight. All the loudspeakers in the city blared the announcement that the very next morning, all previous money notes would be exchanged for new currency printed by the communists. Chaos spread as depositors soon discovered that the exchange rate was set at a ratio of five hundred old piasters to one new dong, the currency of the North. Entire savings were reduced to a fraction of their previous worth. A maximum of two hundred new dong was set for each family, no matter how many piasters were turned in. Whatever balance remained was confiscated by the communists. Families were afterward required to keep most of their savings in banks and were only permitted to withdraw it under certain circumstances, such as serious illness, death in the family, or weddings.

The wealthy were required to go directly to the banks to exchange their currency. Large suitcases laden with piasters were reduced to a billfold's contents. Because of the short notice, a great deal of money was never exchanged in time and became worthless. For some, the demands were too much to bear, and they committed suicide.

Sister Vy, with most of her wealth confiscated and her life in shambles, eventually retreated into her own world and avoided contact with her oppressors. A very sensitive woman of delicate manner, she could no longer endure the personal oppression from the new regime or the pain and suffering around her. The once financially secure countess who translated the Book of Mormon ultimately moved away from Saigon and lived the life of a hermit. She pretended to be a solitary Buddhist nun and lived by herself in an abandoned tiger den with only a sheet of tin laid over the entrance to protect her from the world outside. This was all done so the authorities would no longer bother her. Many others of all classes sought various forms of escape, including taking their own lives, in preference to life under the communists.

The Saigon Saints, along with the rest of the city, suddenly found themselves without enough money to go to market. The diet of many families was reduced to rice and salt. Then even obtaining rice became a difficult task, as more and more was sent to the North. Each family was issued a ration book. Local authorities were given charge of the families and determined the number of coupons in the book. Ironically, much of the rice had been sent over by the United States just before Saigon fell. Soon, other items, like sugar, coffee, and gasoline, were rationed as well. Before long, we needed a coupon or a permit to accomplish just about anything.

Time thus passed by without any new opportunity to escape. Dr. Nghia and I were under increased pressure from the repeated communist directives to report to camp. We began to reconsider our position. We began to feel that perhaps, just to be safe, we should go to the camp for ten days and get it over with. Then we would be free to plan our escape without worrying about the authorities. With this in mind, Dr. Nghia and I prepared ourselves to submit to the so-called reeducation. Just prior to reporting, we learned of an organization in Vung Tau, about eighty miles from Saigon, which could, for a price, help people escape by boat. In fifteen days, they would be ready to take another group out. With this knowledge, we experienced a surge of renewed faith that we would find a way to safety and that I could be reunited with my family. It seemed reasonable to believe that when ten days of reeducation camp were accomplished we could return home and use the remaining five days to finalize our escape plans. But in my conquered homeland, what seemed reasonable was not necessarily what actually happened.

As part of my preparations to go to camp, I tried to establish contact with the outside world. Throughout my travels to Ca Mau and back and in my private thoughts, my mind continually visualized my precious Lien and my dear, sweet children. I wanted her to know that I was alive and that I was going to make an attempt to escape. Communications to anywhere outside Vietnam were restricted. All methods of communication between Vietnam and the United States were severed. This remained a problem for most of the next decade. If a person had contacts in a third country, especially in Asia, as I did, who could pass a coded message on to another person in America, the communication embargo could be circumvented. I was successful in getting a brief cable out of Saigon on May 27. I sent the following to President Wheat in Hong Kong with the assumption that he would know where my family had been taken: "INFORM FAMILY BP TRY TO SEE YOU. TAY." This was my way of saying I was alive and would try to escape. I had no way of knowing if my message was received. Meanwhile, my memory still burned with thoughts about my family. I sent another cable to President Wheat on June 6, which said: "PLEASE INFORM ME IMMEDIATELY OF LIEN TO MY HOME ADDRESS. NEED HELP. BP TAY." I received a response from President Wheat the same day: "LIEN AND FAMILY FINE WITH CHURCH. WHAT HELP NEEDED? WHEAT." I was relieved and pleased with the news. As for President Wheat's question about what help was needed, I hardly knew where to start, but I thought to myself that a helicopter would be nice.

CHAPTER 9

The Reeducation of Tay

Uplifted by fresh assurance that my family was safe and under the watchful care of the Church, I was now prepared to face my ten-day reeducation. Dr. Nghia and I reported to the reeducation camp on June 9, 1975, forty days after the fall of Saigon. Dr. Nghia and I were soon separated. Because he was a medical doctor, he hoped to find favor as one who had saved lives rather than taking them. It was not to be. Since Dr. Nghia had treated soldiers opposing reunification and enabled them to return to duty and kill soldiers from the North, he too must be reeducated. He was assigned to one camp and I to another. There were six or seven separate reeducation camps in the Saigon area, all former military facilities. On June 12, 1975, I was transferred from our original check-in location at the Faculty of Letters School in Saigon and sent to Ong Nam Fortress, located in a rural area about twenty miles east of the city. The official fortress name is Thanh Ong Nam, meaning the "Fortress of Mr. Five," referring to the fifth child, a son, of some important ruler in days gone by. Upon arriving at Mr. Five's, I found some five thousand other poor souls who had also chosen to obey the command to report.

The section of the sprawling fortress where the reeducation camp was laid out consisted of facilities formerly occupied by the Engineering Agency of South Vietnam's military. The Engineering Agency was devoted to manufacturing construction materials made of steel and other metals for military use in buildings, bridges, and equipment. There were many abandoned buildings that formerly served as barracks, warehouses, shops, and offices for the Engineering Agency. To protect these facilities from the North, the South Vietnamese had constructed a large moatlike ditch that tanks and other vehicles could not cross. There were chain-link fences along the moat with guard towers every one hundred feet. The interior of the fortified area was further divided by chain-link fences into six separate sections. All of the fences were covered with vines and other greenery so that visual observation of another section was difficult except at occasional gaps in the vegetation.

About half of the five thousand men who reported to Mr. Five's remained there, and the rest were assigned to other locations. Those of us who remained were organized into six smaller groups of 405 men each. Each such group was confined to one of the six sections, which measured about five acres. The guard towers loomed above us around the outside perimeter of the reeducation camp. A single guard with an AK-47 automatic rifle was stationed in each tower with orders to shoot anyone attempting to cross the fences. The fortifications constructed by the South Vietnamese to keep the North Vietnamese out of the fortress were thus used by the North to keep the officers and leaders of the South in the reeducation camp.

Mr. Five's six smaller camps of 405 men each were further divided, military style, into three companies of 135 each, which were divided into three platoons of 45 each. Platoons consisted of three squads of 15 men each. Forty-five men slept in one

COMMUNIST FACILITY BUILT BY POLITICAL PRISONERS, OUTSIDE SAIGON
(photograph courtesy Allen C. Bjergo)

barracks; a company of 135 men used one kitchen. The groups of fifteen were small enough to maintain personal contact and to control each member; the communists were then able to monitor each individual's reeducation. During my time at the camp, my companions and I were forced to live, work, eat, and fulfill all of our bodily needs within such groups.

The communists preferred to label the smallest groups "units" and used every opportunity to compel us to gain a "unit mentality." We were required to learn and recite mindless slogans and repeat them aloud on demand. Throughout the day we were ordered to shout these messages at the top of our voices to insure that our minds would not drift back to the forbidden practices we had committed prior to the fall—such as thinking for ourselves. Fear encouraged prompt memorization. One slogan was simply "Work in group, eat in group." No explanation was offered; only obedience was required. Disobedience brought swift and awful reprisals, ranging from brutal beatings to solitary confinement in an iron box that resembled a dumpster. We were thus taught what manner of men we ought be in order to get along in our reunified country. I listened carefully and sought to do nothing to offend those in charge over me.

Ten days came and went with no word on when we were to be released. A month passed. It became apparent that my reeducation would take some time. The uneventful three-day reeducation camp for the enlisted personnel was just a deception used to gain the confidence of the officers so they would willingly report for their punishment. As this realization dawned on me, I felt like a pitiful fly that had foolishly flown into the web of a spider. Dr. Nghia and I were not the only Saigon Saints in the web. Colonel Chau and Brother Que, one in the military and one a government official, languished together in another camp for eight years. Brother Thach also spent several years in a camp for his open association with American servicemen and for his desire to worship God openly. Even in prison, he humbly and discreetly taught his prison mates and even some of the guards about the gospel of Jesus Christ.

Many of the male branch members reported to camps and suffered similar fates. Others were spared. My friend and second counselor, Le Van Kha, who was the manager of a large maternity hospital in Saigon, was not deemed to be sinful, because he was engaged in an effort to care for newborn babies and their mothers. I was relieved to know before I came to prison that my old friend would be safe in the new order of things. When the branch dissolved, Brother Kha held services for himself inside his closet at home. Every Sunday thereafter for over a decade, he faithfully blessed and partook of the sacrament of the Lord by himself. If bread was not available, he used grains of rice or the peelings of potatoes. His family, disillusioned with the Church after the fall, took no part in his weekly devotions.

Cao Minh obeyed my counsel not to report, and he was also spared from a lengthy stay at reeducation camp. He grew uneasy staying alone at my home, however, when Dr. Nghia and I did not return as planned. After two months, he assumed we would not be coming back anytime soon. He left my home and traveled west to the Mekong Delta, where the river emptied into the South China Sea. He found work there as a fisherman and patiently waited for his opportunity to sail to freedom.

Escaping by boat was not an easy task. Many voyages in those days were one-way trips, so the supply of boats constantly dwindled. Bad weather and bad luck could easily thwart any attempt to escape. The boat carrying a Saigon Saint sister and her teenage daughter was intercepted at sea by Thai pirates. The boat was robbed and the women were brutally raped. Their boat, unlike most others that encountered pirates on the high seas, eventually reached friendly shores. One of Brother Tran Van Long's daughters, Anh, tried to escape by sea, but her boat was turned back by a North Vietnamese patrol boat. She was apprehended and sent to a reeducation camp for women in the North, where she suffered greatly for merely desiring to be free. It has been calculated that only one-third of the Vietnamese "boat people" successfully escaped, and even then they were often confined for years at refugee camps before obtaining their freedom. Another one-third were caught by communist patrols and forced to return and face whatever punishment was meted out. The final third died from drowning after the accidental sinking of their overloaded boats, or they were attacked by Thai pirates, who typically robbed everyone, killed the men, and sold the women into slavery at Asian brothels. The debauchery and inhumanity of those days knew no bounds.

In one form or another, all of the Saigon Saints suffered varying degrees of deprivation; they languished in poverty and in many cases lacked even basic necessities. Whether in prison, in refugee camps, or at home waiting for a husband or father to return from reeducation camp, all were cut off from former friends and family and from the Saigon Branch. Who is to say which trial was more difficult? For the time being, I walked alone down my own pitiful path. I knew nothing about any other Saigon Saint. I was left to merely speculate, pray, and wonder about everyone else.

When we arrived at Mr. Five's, anything that could be carried away by the retreating army or opportunistic citizens was already gone. Among the missing items were the beds in the barracks, all office furniture, and the toilets, which, as in the case of the homes near our branch, had been ripped from the floors. Because of this, the former military facility was not equipped to handle so large a group. In fact, there were only three working toilets for the three companies in our camp of 405 men. Within two days, they became overused and hopelessly clogged. I had to close my eyes and hold my breath to even enter the building and then try to get out before being overcome by the fumes.

Our captors did not want to share their facilities or water with us, so we were forced to dig deep latrines to handle our bodily waste and also dig wells to obtain our water. We had no shovels, no hammers, no gloves, and no tools of any kind. We had to improvise tools from the materials at hand. Scraps of steel were used as hoes, shovels, and hammers. In some cases, we simply used our bare hands and ingenuity.

Our platoon dug a well thirty feet deep to obtain water. We dug with our hands and scraped the earth with sticks and small pieces of steel. When the hole got wider and deeper, as we had no ladder, we made steps out of the dirt on the sidewall of the well so we could climb in and out. We carried out dirt by the handfuls or piled it on a flat piece of aluminum and carried it out of the pit. After a week or two of digging, we finally penetrated the water table. The well water was adequate at first but was soon polluted, as we had no means of covering the well. The same water had to be used for cooking and washing as well as drinking. Because the water could not be kept free of contaminants, many people developed dysentery and other illnesses.

When it rained, the hole for the latrine would fill up and become a sea of maggots. When the toilet paper we brought with us was gone, we gave our guards money to buy us some more. They obtained some but did not understand the purpose of the rolls of paper. When they found out, the camp authorities declared toilet paper to be an example of the corrupt excesses of imperialism and banned it throughout the camps. We were instructed instead to use our hands and a container of water to clean ourselves. The only containers available to us were our milk powder cans that we had brought with us as part of our initial ten-day food supply. We were compelled to eat, drink, and clean ourselves from the same can. These are just a few examples of the lowliness and degradation heaped upon us in an effort to smother our human spirit.

Activities such as digging wells, cooking food, and taking care of our personal needs did not interfere with putting in a long day of hard labor in the forests. When we were not working in the forests, we worked on the farms. Most of our number came from the city and were unaccustomed to such labor. It was hot and strenuous. It was not unusual for a man to collapse with exhaustion, even though it might bring some form of punishment.

For the first few months of camp, we slept on the cement floor of our barracks. Some platoons, such as those in former warehouses, had floors of dirt. Our captors decided we should construct our own beds. They were not concerned about our sleeping comfort but simply enjoyed dreaming up new ways to punish us. They forced us to haul by hand very heavy one-inch slabs of steel, four feet wide by eight feet long, left over from the Engineering Agency materials. We also had to haul four-by-six-inch steel support girders about fifteen feet long. Our group of fifteen struggled to carry each steel slab and each support beam the one hundred yards or so from the Engineering Agency shops to our barracks. This was extremely difficult and physically exhausting. It took an entire day to move one piece of steel to our barracks. It took the combined strength of ten or more men to get it off the ground and carry it. We carried a steel slab about three or four feet at a time and then had to rest our strained muscles. It ripped the skin on our hands and strained to the maximum every muscle and bone in our bodies.

Being small and frail, I was of little help in carrying steel. If the slab fell flat on the ground, it was very difficult to lift up again, so we let it down on one edge and balanced its weight upright while we rested. The others had mercy on me, and I was permanently assigned to be one of those who kept the slab upright while the others rested and was thus relieved from having to carry it. The beams were almost as difficult to move and presented a different set of challenges. Sometimes they were carried with our group stretched along the length of the beam, all working in unison to inch it along to the barracks. Sometimes the post was lifted at one end, raised upright and allowed to fall forward toward our destination. Both methods worked, but neither worked well. The steel was simply too heavy to move without extraordinary effort. That's why it was still there. The scavengers and looters who took the beds and the toilets as Saigon fell could not budge the steel. We were forced to do what others found impossible.

The beams we carried to the barracks were laid out lengthwise, end to end, along the walls of one side of the building. Another line of beams was laid parallel about seven feet away. The slabs were then laid in place on top of the beams. The process was repeated along the opposite wall. We thus ended up with two long rows of beds, one on each side of our barracks, with a large aisle in between. We slept on the straw mats we brought with us and used the bags in which we carried our ten-day supplies as pillows. Our heads were toward the wall and our feet toward the feet of those opposite. All our worldly possessions, the items we brought with us to camp, were stored at the head of our beds.

During this long, tedious, and painful process, we were in no hurry. There is a Vietnamese saying that by consistent labor, given enough time and patience, one might file a rough piece of steel into a fine needle. We were as persons filing one stroke at a time. After all our extreme struggles, we each had a durable bed of steel that afforded no added comfort whatsoever. The one notable difference was that the rats ran under our beds instead of over our bodies as we slept.

Most of the daylight hours in the camp were divided between studying political lessons and performing hard labor. Our camp's primary labors were cutting trees in the forest and growing crops to provide food. We were told this was to provide for the deprived people in the North, but it was really just another form of punishment. If our captors were so anxious to provide things for the North, they would have provided us with tools so that a much greater quantity of things could be provided. Since we had no tools, the fruits of our labors were meager when measured against our extreme efforts.

We had to fashion a crude saw out of the materials available. It barely functioned; it was more of a scraper than a saw. We worked it back and forth across the bark and into the tree, removing at best a few millimeters of wood at a time. It took our crew of fifteen a full two days of extreme effort to cut down a single tree. The actual production was not important to our captors. Their only interest was the amount of effort it required to produce it. The effort, of course, was designed to bind us as a cohesive unit, dependent on one another to accomplish the task. It is the way of communism, where one individual is not allowed to be above another. This is why the communist system so often fails. It has been accurately said that communism is a system where the people pretend to work and the government pretends to pay them. The end result is that productivity is insufficient to support the group and it eventually collapses. I was free to think such things but not to say them.

Some lessons came with a high cost. Merely to illustrate a point, the price of reeducation was all too often someone's life. A person speaking against communism was confined to the iron box in the scorching sun for a day or two or, in the case of an attempted escape, for a week at a time. The hapless prisoner was fed by his comrades from his unit of fifteen through a hole in the side of the box. His air came through small holes at either end. If he was strong and the weather cooperated with cooling rain and mild nights, he usually survived the ordeal. Many of the old and weak and even some of the strong did not. The sun slowly baked them in their dumpster oven. Two or three days at 150 degrees turned them from defiant patriots into delirious, broken men who died with an unconscious whimper of relief on their parched, dry lips.

The point at which we knew we would be staying in camp a long time was when our captors announced we would have to grow our own food. They said it was not right that the government generously feed us while we were being punished for our sins against the people. We must help provide for ourselves and not be such a burden on the state. In fact, we were already providing for ourselves. We ate well for the first ten days. After what we had brought with us was exhausted, our diet was never adequate. A cup of cooked rice per person per meal was our typical ration; anything else was a bonus.

In my platoon, in the early months of camp, anything edible was fair game. Our barracks was infested with rats that moved about at night. My hungry comrades waited quietly for them to come and then tried to club them or capture them for food. Snakes, lizards, and insects were likewise devoured by the hungry. I was hungry, but I would not eat the rats. Snakes were bad enough, but rats were much too repulsive for my taste. Just as my small size made me a small target in combat, it made my stomach easier to satisfy in the reeducation camp. My food intake needs were small compared to those of others. If I felt extremely hungry, I knew that my companions were feeling it even more.

The Lord blessed me in that my associates took pity on me because of my size. They tried to shield me from the most taxing work when possible, and they decreased the time I spent in hard labor by allowing me to be the cook for our company of 135 men. Cooking was not considered hard labor but was difficult nonetheless. Each group of 135 had a kitchen which had three ovens made of earth and mud. The kitchen had a roof but was open around the sides like a picnic pavilion. Meals were usually consumed in the barracks. Turning the meager portions of rice supplied to us along with the meager vegetables we grew into a useful meal for 135 souls required cooking skills beyond my abilities. I did my best and improved as time went on. I was also in a position to silently ask for the Lord's blessing on the food, that it would bring the men the health and strength they needed to perform their labors and survive their ordeal. My company approved of my efforts, so I remained a cook for my company throughout my stay.

I tried to follow the golden rule in camp, to do unto others as I would have them do unto me. Most of the cooks at Mr. Five's used the dirt-covered chunks of salt with which they were provided just as they came. Using the unprocessed salt resulted in food contaminated with dirt. I took time to separate the salt from the dirt by boiling it in water first. I skimmed away the dirt as it came to the surface and boiled the water away until there was only salt left in the pot. I collected the mostly pure salt and used it in my cooking. Salt was essential to make the leafy greens we ate more palatable. Occasionally, we were provided with large turnips resembling sugar beets. I also used my clean salt to prepare a brine solution in which I soaked thinly sliced pieces of turnips. This preserved the slices over many days so the turnips could be enjoyed over a period of time. My company appreciated this extra effort and rewarded me with kindness and a helping hand in my other labors.

The method of meal preparation was that everything to be consumed for the meal was dumped into the same enormous pot and served to everyone. The pot was about three feet tall and sat on top of the oven. To stir the rice, I had a long paddle as big as an oar from a rowboat. Like my rifle, my paddle was as tall as I was. I had to stand on stacks of wood or on the side of the oven to be able to reach into the pot and stir. Because of this, I often left this duty to others taller and stronger than I.

Rice, the largest part of our diet, was hard to prepare in this manner, because much of it would either remain uncooked on the top of the pot or burn on the bottom. The food was divided into three portions, one for each platoon, and then further divided at the barracks of each group. After many days of such provisions, some of our number refused to eat and as a result began to suffer. In my unit, we sometimes cooked rice portions individually in our milk powder cans. They were placed on the heat of the oven, which was so hot the water in the little cans came to a boil in two or three minutes. The ovens were heated by wood supplied from the forest. The heat from the oven combined with the heat of the sun was at times unbearable. Hard labor was preferable to being the cook in the eyes of many.

The biggest problem with cooking was that there was never enough food. A nagging fear began to creep through the camp as we began to understand the true nature of our condition. Declining weight and poor health were physical evidence that some of us were not going to survive. Since I did not require as much food as the others did, I was fortunate that my weight loss and amount of sickness was less in comparison to those of my associates.

Along with the rice we were provided, we grew a vegetable somewhat akin to spinach. To make this vegetable edible required cooking it in a salt solution. This is where my salt-from-dirt separation was appreciated.

Being able to adapt to whatever food was available was a continual challenge. During a three- or four-month period when rice supplies were short, we were given wheat flour as a substitute. At first, we tried to cook the flour like rice by making balls of dough and cooking them in boiling water. This proved most unsatisfactory. A former baker in our company suggested we construct an oven of steels scraps and bricks and bake bread. We built an oven and then experimented with many different recipes and techniques for baking bread. Guided by the former baker's memory and skills, we eventually produced hundreds of good-quality loaves of French-style bread. About the time our skills peaked, the rice supply was restored, and we no longer had wheat flour for bread.

On rare occasions, we were given some meat or fish. The reaction among prisoners to the tiny morsels of meat was pitiful. That which was given to us was terribly spoiled but would nevertheless be eaten by those who could no longer bear their hunger. Then, as often as not, they would become violently ill with food poisoning. The wise dared not eat spoiled food.

On still rarer occasions, some meat would be provided which was edible, but in such small quantity as to be ludicrous when divided among 135 people. One day, we were given a single chicken to divide. Once again, this was not an act of kindness but a means of punishment. The despair among us overcame reason, and this was the reaction the communists had been hoping for. Some in our company wanted to fight for a part of the chicken; others wanted to draw lots. Usually strong and faithful allies in our struggle for survival, we were now presented with a single chicken capable of driving a bloody wedge between us. There is no way to divide a chicken into 135 meaningful morsels. To avoid further conflict, we decided to grind the chicken into a fine powder and put it in the pot with the meager vegetables we had been given. We thereby remained on friendly terms with one another.

Close friendships were difficult to form and even harder to maintain. No unnecessary talking was allowed in classes and was discouraged the rest of the time. No organizing of any sort was knowingly permitted, and violators were reassigned to different groups to prevent fraternities from developing. I nevertheless developed friendships with some of the men I was first assigned to be with. Two such men were named Hien and Phuong. We were of the same mind and temperament on matters important to us, such as freedom and morality. Even when we were separated into different companies, we could still talk discreetly as we walked along the fences that separated the companies. We shared rumors and critiqued our latest escape ideas. Two or three trusted friends were sufficient. The camp was infested with informants who loved to report subversive activities—such as talking about unapproved subjects—in order to gain favors like extra food or less taxing work assignments. To be safe, I limited what I said to others. I tried to keep my record spotless so that I might be released sooner than those who had extra time added because of infractions to the rules. We knew we could have extra time added, but we had no idea what it was added to. We were only told that we would be released when our reeducation was complete. Our captors would decide when that time came.

The communists that oversaw the camp were from both North and South Vietnam. The South Vietnamese were kinder than their brothers to the North. Those from the North were excessively strict and mindlessly followed every party line. The essence of their philosophy was represented by two words: *Work, I*. This is interpreted to mean the relationship that exists between ourselves and others as a collective society of humanity. Initially we were indoctrinated with several months of intensive study to reshape our thinking. After that, we had periods of several months at a time devoted exclusively to hard labor. Once the labor was completed, we would return to our studies.

Each study period consisted of eight to ten lessons, each of which took a week to discuss. The method of teaching required that the lessons begin early and take at least eight hours to complete. The lessons would be initiated by a discussion about the topic, followed by a confession by each person in turn. This confession was to contain all the sins we had committed against the communists. Such sins were not confined to any particular area at first and included any wrong act we had ever committed.

It seems incredible that the communists would treat matters in such a religious context; nevertheless, they thrust their "religion" upon us with the zeal of a Bible-thumping minister, and we dared not fail to pay attention. Our motivation to cooperate was simple fear. The communists had absolute power over us. At any moment and for any reason we could be exterminated in much the same way as an annoying insect. In extreme cases, outright executions were carried out in full view of the camp, but they were rare. The iron box was not. It was never empty for long. Someone would always offend the communists in some unintended way. There was no trial and no jury; nothing resembling justice was offered or even possible. Offenders were swiftly punished by the offended.

In my case, I had eagerly left my battlefield duties to avoid the continual carnage and thereafter spent my time peaceably teaching English. My conversion to a peaceful life was good, but the communists found fault with this endeavor. They reasoned that by teaching other military members how to speak English, I had aided in their learning how to use American methods to resist the reunification of the country. My crime was that some of my students later learned how to fly fighter planes and dropped bombs on the liberating forces from the North. Since I had helped prepare them, their crimes became my crimes, and their sins became my sins.

No one could escape his sins against the communists. If your sins were hard to discover, they would provide some for you. Even if the esteemed Brother Kha had been at my camp, my captors would have said the babies he helped care for at the maternity hospital grew up to be soldiers that killed brave liberators from the North, so he must therefore share in their sins. With the communists, it was an endless circle of sins for which you could never be fully absolved.

How grateful I was for my true Redeemer and His sacrifice for my actual sins so that I need not face such faulty reasoning at my final judgment! I continually prayed to Heavenly Father, thanking Him for preserving my life in one breath and begging for my deliverance in the next. I was comforted that if I died in this prison, I had done my best, and I hoped it would be sufficient to secure eternal life. My problem was like that of many others. I wanted to go to heaven, but I did not want to die to get there—at least not in a prison just twenty miles from my home and thousands of miles from my family.

Even though I was hungry, I always observed fast Sundays by not eating. This allowed me to worship as an individual without fear of reprisal. I had to prove to myself that I, and not the guards, was master over at least one thing. My associates began to look forward to fast Sundays in hopes that they would get my meals. By giving away my food, I made a direct contribution to the poor. The food I ate, I blessed, and I thanked God for his kindness and mercy in sustaining my life. I sometimes offered the sacrament prayers in the solemn recesses of my mind. Because openly performing religious ordinances was not permitted, I always tried to be inconspicuous and discreet in my words and actions, especially those that would reveal my political or religious views to my captors.

It was a terrible sensation to feel my body slowly losing its life, both physically and mentally. The burdens we were called to bear, especially doing hard labor in the forests without adequate nourishment, made us weaker and weaker. The Lord truly blessed me and eased my burdens by moving upon my associates to be compassionate toward me and shield me from those tasks I simply could not do. I also felt somewhat less burdened mentally because I knew that my family was well. I thanked God often for this knowledge and asked Him to continue to watch over my family. I reasoned that some from the Saigon Branch were also detained in the reeducation camps while their wives and children were forced to provide for themselves. I prayed for them and for their families who were living under such great hardship. I was thankful that I was not further burdened during my confinement with worrying about the survival of my family. Even so, due to my weakening condition, I was fearful that I might never see them again. The ugly shadow of malnutrition swept through the camps, followed closely by a multitude of diseases and skin disorders. Many suffered paralysis from beriberi, brought on by insufficient vitamin B_1. Ironically, this is the vitamin found on the outside of rice, our main food. Our rice had the outside layers stripped off.

After just five or six months in camp, I began to feel the numbing presence of beriberi in my own body. Thereafter, my legs were weak and unstable at times. Ironically, medical knowledge was close at hand. At one time, my unit of fifteen contained two medical doctors and a pharmacist. They were helpful in diagnosing a problem but had no access to the medicine or proper diet needed to treat it. One of the doctors once cut his hand, and it became infected. He went to the camp doctor to request some antibiotics. This camp physician told our good doctor to administer to himself by using saliva and honey as an ointment. This man was presented to us as a doctor, but he had no knowledge of modern medicine and techniques. It seemed very strange that men of greater education and abilities were at the mercy of men of such ignorance. Indeed, the entire camp was made up of officers from the Army of the Republic of Vietnam and high government officials. How remarkable that ignorant men had emerged from the jungle after years of primitive living to take control of a modern and educated society and then attempt to reeducate it. The very idea was as frustrating as it was ludicrous.

About ten months into my ten-day reeducation, I realized there was no end in sight. I began to think more and more about escape. Dying in the attempt seemed no worse than dying in the camp. If a time limit had been placed on my detention, I would have had something to look forward to. As it was, I had nothing. I had not heard from my wife or family and did not know for sure if they had heard from me. My faith was tested to the limits of human endurance, but still I would not deny my God nor cease my silent prayers. During this time, I had not heard from one kindred soul beyond the gates of the camp.

When I was in the depths of despair with beriberi, when I could hardly walk or stand up, I found something to sustain me. In these harsh surroundings, a forbidden book, the Bible, came into my hands. It was brought into the camp by one of the Christians in my barracks who, knowing of my faith in Christ, offered it to me for my comfort. It was a Catholic Bible, which contained the extra books of the Apocrypha. I feasted on its pages and drank deeply of its spirit. It was like drinking the pure water from a spring as it came forth from the ground, in contrast to reading communist propaganda, which was like drinking water downstream, where the cattle had sloshed through and ruined its pureness and clarity.

The first book I read was the book of Job. I found comfort that even in great trials, Job's being much greater than mine, there is hope in the Lord for a better day in the future for those who endure. Although I had read the entire Book of Mormon several times, I had never read the entire Bible. I had only read the New Testament and selected scriptures. In the course of the next three months, I read the Bible twice. We were often confined to our barracks when the work was completed and when we were not eating or exercising. In those times, I read. Our instructors and many of the guards had Sundays off, so our burdens were lightened by default. On Sundays, I could read even more. I was in potential danger in doing so because the Bible was not in harmony with the new order and the required way of thinking. However, with my skinny arms, I could slide the Bible far under the head of the steel bed on which I slept. I had confidence that most other arms could not reach it and that the guards were neither strong enough nor ambitious enough to lift my bed to investigate. It was worth the risk to receive so much spiritual comfort and to feel again the beauty of the gospel.

The scriptures I read kept me from weakening. It was like a long letter from God soothing my soul at a time when I was cut off from all contact with the outside world. One day, as quickly as it came into my life, it was snatched away. We were ordered to collect everything that belonged to us and take it to a large open area. I dared not hide the Bible any longer. The guards proceeded to go through all our individual belongings in detail and took anything they thought was not in harmony with the communist way of life. That included every book in our possession. Even though my Bible was confiscated, it had served its purpose. My faith and my resolve were strengthened, and I grew closer in spirit to my Father in Heaven.

From then on, the communists searched our barracks unannounced every month or so to enforce their new rules. When my Bible was no longer available to me, I tried to recite scriptures to myself from memory. One of those most frequently recalled, if only in fragments, was Psalm 23: "The Lord is my shepherd; I shall not want. He maketh me to lie down in green pastures. . . . He restoreth my soul. . . . Yea, though I walk through the valley of the shadow of death, I will fear no evil: for Thou art with me."

If ever there was a valley of death, it was reeducation camp. After the first ten months of weakening, almost every day someone in the camp died. The lifeless corpses were unceremoniously carried away from their beds of steel, or wherever they fell, and were tossed aside like pieces of human debris. The men in the units of the deceased were forced to dig—without shovels—graves in which to bury their comrades. Most of these deaths were senseless in that they could have been prevented with proper medical care or a better diet or the slightest flicker of hope. This thought penetrated my mind as each lifeless body was lowered into the ground and covered with cold earth. During the first year, no families were informed of a loved one's death. Only later, when families were allowed to visit, did they learn of their great loss.

In the forest, on the farm, or in the kitchen, my frail existence moved forward one step at a time. In my heart, I felt that as long as I could work, my worth and personal strength would not be lost. I wanted to be strong enough to be able to escape if the Lord provided me with a way. I wanted to be alert enough to be able to recognize an opportunity when it came. Meanwhile, one day blended into the next, and the months passed mercifully by as the life of a political prisoner became routine.

CHAPTER 10

The Final Year at Mr. Five's

In the second year of our reeducation, staying alive was largely a personal decision. My platoon was strong in regard to mental toughness. We didn't have anyone who simply gave up and died. I can't say the same for others in our camp. After a year of hard labor and no word from families and no hope for release, many simply chose death rather than struggle onward. As I walked through that dreadful valley, the scriptures brought me comfort and occupied my mind with productive thoughts. To keep up my faith was essential. I had to constantly fight negative assaults on my psyche by declaring to God and to myself that my faith in God's ability to deliver me from this evil had been tried and tested in the past and that I had certain knowledge of His power.

As a unit we discreetly fought to maintain our sanity by sharing information. When we could no longer read books, we taught each other the things we knew. I gave lessons in English. Someone else taught German, and another, Russian. Another taught us Spanish, and still another, Chinese. We thus filled our Sundays and other unsupervised time by learning languages or science or business or medicine. Our barracks of forty-five men was made up entirely of educated officers and government officials who collectively had a vast volume of knowledge. Anyone who knew something the others did not was called on to share his knowledge. In this way, our minds were kept active and our thoughts were focused on our futures, when we hoped to put into practical use the new things we learned.

I often wondered about Dr. Nghia and others who reported to camp about the same time I did. There were dozens of military officers in the branch. I knew that those not evacuated must have been facing the same difficulties I faced. There were also nonmilitary priesthood holders who were not evacuated who reported to the camps. What of them? I knew not. Oh, how I longed for the old days in the Saigon Branch! We had found such happiness together. Now, our combined misery was hard to contemplate. In my heart, I hoped my brethren in the gospel had not reported to camp. Or, if they had, that they were released by now. Or, if they were not released, that they were well. Or, if they were not well, that they were alive. Or, if they were not alive, that they were encircled in the loving arms of the Lord.

In my camp, those who did not die suffered nearly as much. Many of us suffered from a skin mite infestation called scabies. This problem is caused by the presence of mites, lots of them, that bore just under the skin, especially around the wrists and ankles. The itching sensation they cause is insatiable. In the hope of receiving some sort of relief, we in the unit who were infected consulted with a doctor who was confined with us. In his most serious and helpful voice, he told us, "The best way to prevent the discomforts of this condition is to stop scratching the affected areas." A few weeks later, the good doctor contracted the same problem himself and was observed scratching himself in a violent manner as he cursed the mites under his breath. We asked him why he didn't follow his own advice. "The only way to relieve the itch is to scratch it," he said. We laughed at the irony of his misery. It felt good to laugh, if only for a moment.

Any bit of humor we could grasp was cherished, but done with care. Sometimes the guards, insecure in their ingrained stupidity, bristled and assumed we were laughing at them. Some chose to punish us with loss of privileges, such as eating, to get even with our good humor. Therefore, laughing in their presence was avoided.

If for some reason we laughed or yelled or showed some other strong emotion during the work period, we would be immediately reprimanded and required to stand at attention for long hours in the hot sun. If provoked at night, a guard would require us to stand at attention all night and not even permit us to relieve ourselves at the latrine.

On one occasion, a comrade and I were deemed too noisy. After using the latrine pit, we were prevented from returning to the barracks. We were ordered to stand in the darkness while the guard "instructed" us throughout the night on various slogans and party lines. At daylight, we were still made to perform our usual labors without having received any rest. Thus fatigued, I felt my body becoming enveloped in pain, both physical and emotional, and I could feel myself beginning to break. The next night another guard began to chastise us for having spoken to the first guard the night before. We had to choose our words very carefully or we would again face punishment. So it went day after day. Even though there were not enough guards to watch everyone, we began to feel like they were watching even when they were not present.

The time came when I could no longer look on my captors as brothers. They were too cruel to be brothers, and they exercised unrighteous dominion in the extreme. I hated and feared and cursed them. They were children of darkness far removed from any knowledge of or allegiance to the God I prayed to for the strength to forgive and love all men. Yes, I forgave them in time, but in those days all I felt for them was the powerless feeling of hate. The British playwright George Bernard Shaw once remarked that although he had never killed anyone, he took great pleasure in reading certain obituaries. So it was with me. I would not have killed the guards, but I would have rejoiced in their demise.

After about a year in camp, we were allowed some visitors. This was a cause for great inner celebration for those who were permitted the privilege. Visiting family members were permitted to bring money, clothing, and food items to us. The guards, for a fee, would buy approved items for us in the nearby town where most of them lived. Clothing was greatly needed by all, since most of us had only one set of clothes that had worn out long ago. Any kind of food was also a welcome gift, especially sugar or honey or anything sweet.

We received many live baby ducks and chickens within our company, and we created a company flock of mixed fowl. We blocked them off along a fence line, where they fed on a never-ending supply of maggots. The flock grew very quickly. When four or five were killed and plucked at once, enough meat was provided to actually taste it and to savor a scattered morsel or two in our meal. These rare occasions were celebrated. It is extremely difficult to adequately explain the agony and sheer drudgery of eating the same thing day after day, month after month. When something new was served, gladness in the heart came with it. Such days were few and far between.

In the beginning, the farm labor brought some measure of hope, because we knew that at some point the food would be harvested and perhaps we would be provided with better nutrition and regain our strength. When the time came when the communists did not want to share the main farm food with us anymore, we were allowed to grow our own. Rice continued to be supplied, but obtaining additional food was deemed to be our own problem.

The communists then allowed each company of 135 the use of an unoccupied plot of ground on which to grow their own vegetables. By the second year, our company plot flourished. The plot was further divided so that each fifteen-man unit had three forty-foot-long rows to cultivate. We shared our crude hoes to weed and cultivate the soil. We grew only the spinach-like leafy greens in our rows. These greens could be snipped off, and they would immediately begin to grow again. Thus, we did not have to keep replanting our garden. We relied on rainwater to nourish our crops. We used the chicken and duck manure from our company flock as fertilizer. We also judiciously used our own ammonia-laden urine. Too much killed a plant, but the right amount made it grow better. Every attempt, however crude, was made to maximize the amount of food produced in the space allotted. If we rotated the harvest times correctly, we always had something ready to eat. It was a lot of work, but whenever the cooking pot was full, it seemed worth it.

In spite of my afflictions and a tired and saddened heart, I did not abandon hope. I felt that one day I would be reunited with my dear wife. Something within continued to say, "Have faith." If I were to stop believing, I would lose my reason for living and I would surely die. With my health history, I should have been dead already. There was never any doubt in my mind that my strength was limited. My resistance would one day come to an end. I desperately pleaded with the Lord to hear my prayers and the lamentations of my heart and come to my aid. All the while, I wondered and worried about the others in the Saigon Branch who had been left behind after the airlift. Had they escaped yet? Were they still alive? Were they keeping the faith? I especially prayed for those who were in the same predicament as I, wasting away in reeducation camps. I prayed for their families also, who faced extreme hardship in maintaining a living without their husbands and fathers. I had faith the Lord would not forget us. I was determined to escape and rejoin my family, but I knew it must happen soon. It would be an upstream journey, and I was weakening day by day. Soon, I promised myself, I would either be free or dead. Or both.

The sad fact was that escape was not difficult, but to remain free was. One only need slip away from a work detail in the forest to escape the camp. The problem was that many guards lived in the vicinity of the camp and were constantly on the lookout for anyone trying to leave without authorization. Bus stops were watched closely, and informers were everywhere, eager to trade their information for special favors. I spent a great deal of time and energy thinking of ways to escape and to avoid capture once outside the camp. Perhaps the thoughts alone helped me the most, for I knew that as long as my mind and spirit could remain free, I could carry on another day. In time, I knew that the Lord would answer my prayers.

I did not discuss escape with my friends, Hien or Phuong, or anyone else until after we had faced severe trials together and I knew the workings of their hearts. To avoid detection, information was passed very slowly over tried and proven

FORMER SITE OF PRISONERS' FARM
(photograph courtesy Allen C. Bjergo)

channels between men who trusted one another with their very lives. My plan of escape involved leaving the group while working in the forest. Sometimes the work area sites would be very remote, forcing us to abandon the trucks and finish our journey on foot. In this brief interlude, our captors were in a weakened position because they could not always keep us in view. One day, before I could use my escape plan, six others from my company escaped in this manner. They were free for two months, and then they were returned to camp for all to see. They were placed in the iron boxes and given little food or water for nearly two weeks, until four died and the others were at the point of death. Then they were released on a "holy day" and given clemency to show how compassionate their captors were—captors, of course, who had inflicted the inhuman treatment that killed four of our comrades.

Sometime later, another group set out to escape and was caught. Some were killed outright, and the others, in a mockery of justice, were spared for a trial. As if to further our reeducation process, we were called upon to be their judges. For those who suggested two or three years be added to their imprisonment, the communists said they had judged improperly and were still blinded by their capitalistic ways and that they themselves required more time in reeducation camp. In this manner, we were compelled to "judge" our friends with harsh criticism and ten years of additional time in prison for their crimes. Once again, the communists sought to divide us against ourselves and lead us by force to the objectives they sought.

These incidents did nothing to dampen my will to escape, but they did serve to temper my efforts. My main objective in the world was to see my wife and children again. If I could convince the communists that my reeducation was complete, being released would be as sweet as escaping. On the other hand, there was no reason to believe that I would ever be released. Sometimes, an influential relative of one of the prisoners would submit a petition or offer a bribe to secure his release. Every day at the formation of prisoners after the five o'clock meal, prisoners would listen for their name to be called. Few ever were, but the hope was there that someone would apply for your release and it would be granted. Therefore, I was constantly torn between being extremely patient and desperately reckless. I gave in to neither. On more than one occasion, when the urge to escape was greatest, I had what I feel was direction from the Holy Spirit. One time in particular, I was plotting in my mind one of my escape plans—to walk away from my work detail and slip into the jungle. Because of my combat experience, I had confidence in my ability to evade the enemy until I could get fresh clothes and blend into the population. I prayed for help and received in my mind a rebuke of my plans. I had the distinct feeling that I should be patient. I recalled the feeling I had had at the last sacrament meeting that all would be well in the due time of the Lord. I decided against attempting to escape at that time. Later, my conscience, or perhaps the adversary himself, would taunt me for being timid and without courage and would urge me to escape. Thus, I continually wavered between patience and recklessness.

Despite writing letters shortly after coming to camp, over a year passed and I had never received a reply. I had no reason to believe my letters were ever sent. In the early months of camp, we were ordered to write letters to our families. We were instructed in the manner that they should be written. They were to be short; they were to say that work was going well, that food and conditions were good, and that we were being treated well by our captors. Letters that did not meet the approval of the communists brought on swift punishment and were rewritten to comply with their requirements. Subsequent letters were not to vary more than a few words from the approved original.

The letters we wrote were not to be mailed immediately, but collected and retained in the camp post office. If our reeducation went well, we were told that one of our letters would be sent. Months later, another might be sent. Most of the letters, according to some trusted guards, were simply burned. We had no knowledge of any of our letters actually being sent until mail began to be received at the camp. The incoming mail was then used as barter by the communists to extract additional confessions. They would say, "We have a letter from your wife. You can have it if . . ." and then present to you impossible conditions, such as perfect behavior for a month or double production on your work assignment. By the end of the first year, I had written two letters, but neither one was sent. I was desperate to make contact with my family.

In my second year in camp, we were permitted to receive a gift of food or clothing from relatives who were finally allowed to come to the camp to visit us. My sister, Ba, came to see me. I was aware of her coming visit in advance. In preparation for her visit, I decided to do a dangerous thing. I decided to attempt to smuggle a letter out of camp to circumvent the camp's nonexistent postal service. I wrote the letter on August 16, 1976, addressed to President Wheat in Hong Kong, with another letter enclosed for my wife. It was my intention that the letter would ultimately be delivered to my wife. I risked my life to write this letter secretly, and I took painstaking care that my intentions would not be discovered so I could give it to Ba and she could take it out of the camp.

Before we could see our relatives, we were subjected to a complete body search. As time neared for my search, I placed the letter under the cloth band inside my hat while they searched those in front of me. To divert their attention, I placed a pen and a pad in plain sight inside the hat and laid it on the ground. Tense moments passed while I tried not to show any indication that I was hiding something. I began to tremble, as I knew any close examination of the hat would reveal its contents. If discovered, I knew that I might be sent special delivery straight to the iron box and left there. After they finished searching my body, their attention was returned to my hat. If ever a prayer needed answering, it was now, when my very life hung in the balance. The guards examined the ordinary pen and pad, and they lost interest in my hat. They let me pass by.

As my sister approached me, I quickly and calmly withdrew the letters from my hat and placed them into her hands. Then we had a sweet reunion. We cried together, and I gratefully accepted her love and good wishes. She also brought me food and a little money. She struggled in her life but survived by her hard labor. She still operated the produce business with the help of her husband and children. All too soon, our visit ended, she was led away, and I returned to my unit. Once safely home, she mailed the letters out of the country—after they had passed the censorship tests, of course.

Here is the text of my letter to President Wheat:

> I have been in the concentration camp for more than fourteen months to be reformed into a good citizen. I always try my best and study well, to labor well with a hope that I will soon be considered as a progressive citizen to be released home.

Enclosed with this note is my letter to my fiancée, Lien. Please send it to her. I haven't contacted her since the revolution succeeded in VN. I know she worries about me very much. I am afraid because of me, she neglects her studies. Would you please encourage and comfort her. I always have a strong faith that if we endure in our faith and pray to our God continuously, without weariness, we will receive a great blessing, a blessing of gathering, someday. I know surely about this.

President, I think you will leave your position for home soon. Before you go, please remember to give my name to the new president and explain to him about my circumstances for possible future help. I pray that God will inspire you in every work. Please give my regards to your family. May God bless you and your family.

Love and prayers,
Nguyen Tay

P.S. I don't know when I go back home, therefore don't write to my address. You may write Sister Ba.

The letters were written in a manner to pass censors so they would be sent out of the country. I pretended that Lien was my fiancée studying abroad and that I supported the revolution. I had the letters sent to Hong Kong and not to the United States. Within the coded messages was the one I wanted to convey. These letters were the first indication to my wife and friends that I was still alive, and they came fourteen months from the time of my telegram prior to entering reeducation camp.

In my message of love to Lien, I dared not mention the camp or anything about the conditions there. I pretended in my letter to be on the outside. I wrote that I had visited the president of the Saigon Branch, who was detained in camp, the same one who had baptized her. Since it was my privilege to baptize her, I knew she would not mistake my situation. I asked her if she remembered him. I said that he sent her his kind regards. I told her that even though he was severed from his family, he loved them still and was always faithful that they would someday be reunited.

Although I wrote three letters from camp, this is the only one my wife ever received. It gave her hope and helped her sustain her faith that we would someday be together.

President Bradshaw delivered the letter personally to my wife after it was forwarded to his Orem, Utah, home by President Wheat. He went to see my wife and listened to her as she translated my letter. They both sat in tears as my fate became known to them. The Spirit renewed the comfort my wife had received previously from President Kimball's promise that we would be reunited.

Six more months passed before my sister was permitted to visit me again. This time she brought me a miracle. It was a letter from my wife. The emotional impact was overwhelming when I beheld that it also contained a picture of my wife and children. My fingers traced their faces; my tears welled up and I got a lump in my throat. My children were growing up without me, and they were so beautiful. Hope and despair swelled within me simultaneously. I felt like laughing and crying at the same time. First, I was overcome with joy at this wonderful blessing of having contact with my loved ones after nearly two years' time. Then, from the depths of my soul, I began to shake, first with despair, then with determination. It was definitely time to leave. It was time to be where God intended for me to be: with my dear wife and precious little ones. My soul cried out for freedom. I prayed earnestly to Heavenly Father, whose power is beyond the iron grip of the communists. My faith and resolve grew each day, and I knew I must regain my freedom or die in the effort. Let this be "the own due time of the Lord," I prayed. I didn't think I could be patient any longer.

During my entire time in prison camp, I thought often about the time the Lord delivered me from my combat duty, where eventual death was inevitable. As I prayed in the jungles for my deliverance in those days, it did not seem possible that I could be singled out from among the masses and be allowed to walk away from the fighting. Still, the Lord, using my language skill, had performed a miracle and taken me from the jungle and placed me within the peaceful walls of the language school. I knew, therefore, that the Lord could deliver me whenever He so chose. It was more than faith. I knew He could. By this time, I had been in prison camp for over two years, and despite the fact that I had an impeccable record, I had no indication my release would ever come. I found myself asking for another miracle. I had been a model prisoner and had carefully chosen my words and actions so as not to offend my captors. I could do nothing more on my own than I had already done to gain my release. I reasoned with the Lord that I had been patient and I had done all that I could do. Now it was up to Him. I placed my final appeal for my freedom in His hands. I prayed mightily for His intercession on my behalf and pleaded with Him to do that which I knew He could do.

After twenty-seven months in reeducation camp, the chance I had prayed for finally came. Two of my father's brothers established contact with my sister, and she told them of my predicament. They agreed to help. My uncles had gone to the North in 1954 when the Geneva Accord between France and Vietnam was signed and were later drawn into the communist movement. One was in a position of prominence. As an officer of the communist government, an administrator of electrical power, he was in a position to help. He filled out the necessary sponsorship papers, including a guarantee document that promised that when I was released he would personally see to it that my reeducation process would be finished. He also had to explain the reason he had not sought me out earlier. There was a program in force that allowed relatives in the North to oversee the reeducation of their kindred in the South, but the time for applications was over. He explained that he was in the service of the people and had to finish his work before he could take the time to teach me. Now, he told them, he was ready to do his duty to his nephew. My sister visited me again at camp and showed me a copy of my uncle's petition on my behalf. My heart swelled with hope, as it had when I applied for language school as a means to escape combat. The very thought of walking out of the camp a free man strengthened my spirit and my heart. My days passed with renewed hope and inward happiness; at night my thoughts were filled with anticipation of my desired reunion with my family.

Behind the scenes, progress was slow. The law established by the communists made my uncle duty-bound to take responsibility for reeducating me, but the authorities said that my uncle had neglected his duty and that I would have to stay in camp to finish my reeducation. My prospects for a quick release were dashed by this decision, but I had no knowledge of it.

Not deterred, my other uncle also petitioned for my release. A second and a third time, both uncles tried to get me released. My former home being unavailable to me, my sister pledged to let me live with her family so that I would not be a burden on society. Finally, my record at the camp was examined, and it was shown that I had worked hard and had shown marked improvement in learning my lessons. In twenty-seven months, I had not been involved in any serious trouble and had received only the routine punishments inflicted on everyone as part of the normal daily activities. My reeducation was considered "well in hand," and my uncles' persistent petitions were taken under consideration. I was not consulted in the matter and knew nothing of the progress being made.

One day, at the regular formation after five o'clock dinner, my name was called with three others. Calling my name could be a good or bad thing depending on the reason I was singled out. I speculated on the possibilities. Sometimes people were sent to other camps. Sometimes they were informed of a special punishment to be meted out for some real or imagined infraction. Sometimes they were released. I was given no reason for being called. I was only told to report to the camp headquarters. There I was informed by the camp commander that my reeducation would be turned over to my uncle and I would be free to leave the camp the following morning. My joy was full. I cried tears of relief and I pledged in my heart my everlasting praise to God in heaven for answering my prayers for deliverance. It seemed almost predictable that my captors, wrongheaded to the end about the men they imprisoned, thought my display of gratitude was directed at them. They carefully instructed me on the conditions of my release as I filled out the necessary paperwork. They told me that after my release from reeducation camp, I was restricted to living in a small area on the outside. In this parole-like arrangement, every fifteen days, I was required to report my activities of the preceding fifteen-day period. The communists made various threats concerning my relatives if I tried to escape. (My uncle later discounted the threats as bravado. He said there was little or no cooperation between the communist chiefs in the villages. They operated within the sphere of their own influence and rarely followed up on directives originating from outside their area.)

Excitement and relief penetrated my very soul as I rejoined my unit for the last time. Men I had worked beside, slept beside, eaten with, and cooked for warmly congratulated me on my good fortune and wished me well. As was the custom in camp, I gave to my comrades in my unit all of my personal belongings, consisting of a little food, a light jacket, my hat, my mat, a notebook and pen, my milk powder can, my travel bag, and assorted small items my sister had brought me. Another custom in camp was that persons who were leaving sometimes carried out messages for the relatives of those close associates left behind. I carried in secret five such written messages to the outside.

My release gave others in my unit a burst of hope that they too would someday be released. After nearly two and a half years of reeducation, the number of men leaving camp alive seemed to be increasing to a steady trickle. I was overjoyed to join the chosen few. I was so overjoyed, I found no sleep that night. My mind raced ahead toward a new life with my family and pondered the many obstacles that blocked my path. The Lord had delivered me from the despair and degradation of reeducation camp, but even as I wept tears of joy through a sleepless night, I recognized that there were mountains left to climb.

As directed, I reported to the camp commander early the next morning. Without ceremony or further discussion, I received my precious papers and walked to the main gate of the camp. I showed the papers to the chief guard. He motioned to another guard with his hand, and the gate opened. I treasured each step forward as I passed by the guards and heard them close the gate behind me with a final farewell clank and rattle of colliding chain link and metal. I turned around and took one last look at my former prison. A flood of prison memories washed over me, and I began to cry tears of joy that I was released and tears of pain for what I had endured. As twenty-seven months of forced confinement ended, the range and depth of my feelings is impossible to adequately express, but the predominant feeling was one of joy. Although I was not yet in the arms of my dear wife, I realized I was one giant step closer.

CHAPTER 11

The Fresh Air of Freedom

I walked a short distance outside the gates of the prison and, using money my sister had brought to me, hired a man to drive me on the back of his motorbike to Ba's home.

It was the most wonderful ride of my life. The fresh air of freedom blew through my hair, streamed against the skin of my smiling face, and dried my tears. The sudden absence of fear, of stench, of flies, of mindless slogans, and of pointless confinement refreshed my soul. The wind from the motorbike ride seemed to blow away my troubles and sweep clean any vestiges of my so-called reeducation. I was still me. My ride to Sister Ba's was an hour of pure joy.

My sister was not at her home when I arrived. She and her husband still earned their living selling produce at the marketplace. One of our cousins went to the market to inform her of my release, and she came home immediately. I ran up the road to meet her as she hurried toward me. We embraced amid tears of joy. Here we were again, honoring our childhood pledge to help each other to the end. Ba's petition to my uncles to help me and their petition to the communists to release me were the basis of my freedom. My only sibling, my devoted sister, had not forgotten me in my time of need. God had used her to open the way to leave reeducation camp.

Ba informed me that half of our former duplex was vacant. I had sold that half of the duplex after I got married and moved to another house. The family that had bought my side of the duplex was no longer in Vietnam. I was thus able to stay in my old house next to Ba and her family. A Saigon Branch member had borrowed the motorbike I had left with Ba, and I soon retrieved it for my own use. I used the motorbike, the same one Airman Moore had given me, to deliver the messages I had secretly carried out of the prison.

I also visited some members of the disbanded Saigon Branch who were still living in their same homes. From them, I learned about a few others. The communist ban on meetings of three or more persons without a permit was still in effect. To my great sadness, no formal meetings had been held, nor could they be, by the branch members during my confinement. I visited Brother Nghia, whose brother assisted us in Ca Mau during our unsuccessful attempt to escape immediately after the fall of Saigon. Brother Nghia had married a young woman, also a member of the Saigon Branch, and they had settled in Saigon. He informed me about some of the other members. Everyone, it seemed, was in desperate straits, drinking the dregs of the bitter cup of poverty. Sister Chau and Sister Que and other wives and families of former branch members were destitute, while their husbands languished in prison. Brother Long's family was haunted by the imprisonment of their daughter, who had attempted to escape Vietnam by boat. Cao Minh had moved to the seaside along the Mekong Delta to become a fisherman. Sister Vy had simply disappeared. Le Van Kha was still working at the maternity hospital but received less income than before and struggled to support his family. In spite of these circumstances, he remained faithful in the Lord. In the flock's scattered circumstances, a meaningful reunion of the branch was not possible. We commiserated over the condition of the branch I once led and the loss of fellowship we once enjoyed.

Some branch members had lost their faith or knew not how to express it. My attempts to visit members were met with little success. Some had moved, some had left Vietnam, and some had died. I visited four sisters who had once been wealthy from their family's large business holdings, some warehouses, and a construction supply business. They lost their wealth and their businesses when their assets were confiscated by the communists. They had maintained their faith but lost contact with most other members. The tangled mess and aftermath of the demise of the Saigon Branch was impossible to untangle at that time.

I learned quickly that being out of prison was a great improvement, but it was not freedom. I could not go where I wanted to go or do what I wanted to do. In fifteen days, I reported my activities as directed to the local communist village chief. His lack of interest in my mundane existence was encouraging. On the twentieth day, I made the very difficult decision to escape at the first opportunity, come what may. I could not accept my life as it was. My loving family awaited my return; I had to make the attempt. Those who had helped me get out of prison had, on paper at least, guaranteed to complete my reeducation. Nevertheless, the dream of seeing my family again was what had enabled me to endure. Knowing that I could not be at peace with myself without my family and aware of my uncle's view that the communist threats were mere bravado, my sister fully approved of my decision.

I made another decision. Even though my limited visits with former branch members were touching and emotional, I sadly realized that the branch, like Humpty-Dumpty, could not be put back together again at that time. Under the circumstances, I felt that my place was with my family, and the Spirit confirmed that to me.

I reasoned that if the Lord wanted me to be with my family, He would provide a way for that to happen. He had delivered me from combat. He delivered me from prison camp. He could deliver me to my family. I decided to pray for a way to leave Vietnam and not cease until I was shown a way. I had no money and no prospects of getting any. I needed a miracle. I turned to the Provider of miracles and pleaded for just one more.

For the next three days and nights, I prayed and pleaded with the Lord to deliver me from Vietnam into the embrace of my family. When I wasn't praying, I was singing. I barely slept. All alone in my former house, I paced and prayed and sang the hymn, "I Need Thee Every Hour," over and over and over again. Never have I so fervently prayed or sung so much as I did those three days.

> I need thee every hour,
> Most gracious Lord.
> No tender voice like thine
> Can peace afford. . . .
>
> I need thee every hour
> In joy or pain.
> Come quickly and abide,
> Or life is vain. . . .

I need thee every hour,
Most holy One,
Oh, make me thine indeed,
Thou blessed Son!

I need thee, oh, I need thee,
Every hour I need thee.
Oh bless me now, my Savior,
I come to thee! (*Hymns,* no. 98)

Faith precedes the miracle. On the third day, Sister Luong, whose family had been baptized by the missionaries, came to my house to approach me privately. She had enough money saved to buy passage for one person out of Vietnam. She selected one of her sons to be that person, and she wanted me to accompany him and look after him in his travels. "Are you willing to risk your life to leave the country on a small fishing boat?" she asked. By this time, I was willing to endure whatever pain or danger was required to escape the bonds that kept me from my family. I was willing to attempt an escape using any means possible, including fishing boats. I looked at Sister Luong, through my tears of gratitude to my God, and said simply, "I am willing." From that moment there was no turning back.

My mind drifted back to my ten-day lookout perch at Cape Ca Mau and how I had given up hope after no ships were sighted. I thought of the escape plan that Dr. Nghia, Cao Minh, and I were going to use just five days after our ten-day reeducation camp was completed. I had always thought how foolish I had been for letting those opportunities slip by! Or was I? I knew that the waters were more heavily patrolled just after the fall and were thick with pirates. I could not be sure I would have made it back then. Perhaps the hand of the Lord had slowed me down for some wise purpose. I was alive, at least, even though I had had to pass through twenty-seven months of unspeakable misery. I seemed to be right back where I had started, only I was much weaker physically and I was totally without funds. But I was alive, and I was being provided another chance "in the Lord's own due time." I did not second-guess the Lord. I felt only gratitude as another prayer was answered.

Sister Luong made the necessary arrangements, including contacting the boat owner so I could meet with him and the others who were planning to go. Without the consent of all, I would not be permitted to join them. My greatest concern was that I had no money. I told Sister Luong to ask if I could possibly pay after we left the country. This concerned her, but she said she would try to work something out. Days passed as I anxiously awaited word, hoping that it would come before I had to report my activities to the authorities again.

After several days, I was taken to meet with the organizers of the escape project. They knew very little about me or my background in the Church. They understood that I would not be accompanied by my wife and children, which made the issue of "sail now, pay later" more palatable, since I required little space. At this council, I was inspired to appeal to them logically. I boldly declared that my help would be more valuable than gold to them. I spoke English and I had American contacts in Hong Kong through the Church, which would be of great value to them when we arrived in Thailand. I also told them that through my family or my church, I was certain I could get sponsors for all of them. Having a sponsor would result in a shorter stay at our refugee center. The entire group except for Sister Luong's son and myself were Vietnamese

Catholics. They were wealthy and had ample gold; money was not a major concern. Their concern was that they had already made two attempts to escape that had failed. The added incentives I offered appealed to them and gave me hope that I would be accepted into the group. They counseled among themselves and unanimously agreed to include me. I nearly wept with excitement and thanksgiving as I received the solid approval of this goodly band of freedom seekers. In soberness and secrecy, we made a pact to sail together to our collective destiny in three days' time. This voyage did not promise success, but I would have the chance I had been praying for since the day the American helicopters stopped flying and communist tanks rolled into our city. The next three days passed quickly.

On October 6, 1977, we began our dangerous journey. The plan I was permitted to take part in had been years in preparation and was well conceived. Still, there were many risks. There would be twenty-four people on our boat. Except for Sister Luong's son and me, all of the men, women, and children on the boat belonged to two large families. So many people on a small boat, especially the children, would surely arouse suspicion. Measures would have to be taken to avoid being checked.

At about two in the afternoon, we boarded two small boats that would take us to a rendezvous point with the larger vessel that we would be using. To avoid detection, I disguised myself as a mechanic. I wore military pants like those used by most laborers of the time. I also wore a dirty, grimy shirt to enhance my image as a mechanic. The clothes on my body were my only possessions; all else had to be abandoned. My life and my chance for freedom were all I needed at that time. To help with the plan, in case our group was stopped, I had to memorize the addresses and other personal information that a person of my pretended profession would be expected to know. All of us could recite stories for who we were and why we were on the river at this time and place. Our plans were laid with the utmost caution. I was happy that we did not have occasion to test them under fire. After a tense, two-hour journey, we arrived safely at the second boat and quickly boarded. The larger vessel was moored at the Long Ans River, about thirty miles west of Saigon.

Just after boarding the larger boat around four o'clock, the group requested me to offer a vocal prayer for our safety and success. We all knelt down in humility in the fish hold of the boat, and with freedom in the balance, I offered a prayer to Heavenly Father that all of us might be safely delivered from our trials and find the freedom we sought. Three of our group then went topside to pose as fishermen while the rest of us remained in the fish hold. The boat was old and its seaworthiness was questionable. Nevertheless, I was as happy as Noah was with the ark. God willing, this would be our ark, our deliverance from the political storms, our safe passage to freedom.

As we began our journey, our first problem was looking like a normal fishing party. Most fishing boats like ours carried a crew of three or four, but there were twenty-four persons on our little fishing boat. As we sailed downstream toward the ocean, only three persons were visible on the stern of the twenty-foot-long craft, while twenty-one of us quietly hid below deck in the fish hold. The strong smell of fish filled my nostrils, and I ached from my uncomfortable position, smashed on every side by bodies stuffed like sardines below the deck. Those on deck attempted to act very normal as we sailed down the river toward the sea, moving at a normal pace with the other river traffic.

At a critical place in the river, just before it emptied into the sea, we had to pass a well-guarded watchtower. This passage point had been observed in advance by those planning the escape. They had discovered that the guards had a tendency to check several boats at once when they were suspicious or in the mood to investigate. At other times they sat lazily at their posts and checked no one. Our plan required that we pass by unchallenged because they would easily discover us if we were stopped for a routine check or due to suspicion. We would all be killed or imprisoned. If we made a run for it, communist gunboats would easily overtake and destroy us. Part of the escape plan was to use another boat to test their mood. If it was boarded, we would abort our attempt. If it passed by, we would attempt to do likewise.

As we approached the guard post, we had to time our passage at precisely the right moment. The other boat had to be close enough to observe but far enough away that we could divert our course if necessary. All aboard were keenly aware of our dangerous predicament. Those of us below deck, though uncomfortable and to the point of nausea, kept absolutely still, so that the pounding of our hearts was all we were conscious of. Right on schedule, the other boat came from the opposite direction and passed the tower moments before we did. My prayers were answered as the decoy boat sailed through without incident.

Now it was our turn. Our greatest concern now was that we were heading out to sea at a time when most fishermen were returning for the day. Even though the other boat had passed by, we could still be singled out for investigation. We closed in on the spot where vessels were either stopped or allowed to pass by. Nerves were on edge as our boat came alongside the guard tower and was completely exposed to communist guns. The guards had an open view of our vessel. We were watched but not stopped. Smoothly and silently, our little shuttle boat to freedom glided by the tower.

As we left the river channel and began to hit the waves of the ocean, we breathed a fish-flavored sigh of relief. We had cleared our first major hurdle. Below deck, the smell in the fish hold was becoming overwhelming. The sealed hatches cut off any fresh air that might enter; it seemed as if we were suffocating. I felt like Jonah inside the great fish waiting to be spat out into the fresh air. The ocean waves caused the boat to bounce and bob like a discarded bottle. Before long, everyone below deck was ill, and our misery was compounded. Further out in the ocean, the seas were calmer. Still, moments seemed like hours in our pathetic state. We dared not emerge from the hold for fear of being discovered by communist patrol boats or planes that continually skimmed these waters in search of freedom seekers attempting to leave the country. I realized that by simply leaving, our little group was reaffirming our opposition to the adversary's plan of denying us our agency, and we were also defying his desire to compel us to be miserable like unto himself.

Late that first night, around midnight, after eight long, miserable hours below deck, we felt it was reasonably safe and finally went out on the deck to revive ourselves. Never has a breath of fresh air felt so good on my face or in my lungs. We spontaneously shouted for joy. We were actually on our way to freedom, and our hopes were riding sky-high.

We set a course southward with the intent to eventually turn west toward safe havens in Thailand. Our course, of necessity, took us past Con Son Island, now a communist base of operations. As we passed by late at night with other legitimate fishing vessels, we felt we could avoid detection. We were wrong. Suddenly, about two in the morning, we were spotted from a distance by a communist patrol boat. When we were challenged by bullhorn and ordered to stop, we turned away and traveled full speed ahead into the darkness to escape the searchlights. We turned off all our lights, and since we could not outrun a patrol boat, we cut back on our engines and sloshed along in near silence, gliding slowly and ever deeper into the darkness, with only the sounds of the ocean around us. I hoped the bright canopy of stars and muted light of the moon were insufficient to betray our position. We all feared being fired upon and sunk, as sinking the refugee boats had become the favored solution of the communists. They did not fire indiscriminately when they first spotted us for fear of hitting a legitimate fishing vessel, but if they spotted us now, there would be no holding back. For three long hours they attempted to find us. Their spotlights pierced the night and reflected on the calming waters. We could see them plainly at times because of their searchlights, but they could not see us. As the hours passed, the distance grew between us. When the lights disappeared entirely, we powered up the engines and slipped farther into the dark.

We were fortunate enough to avoid detection, but we were forced many miles off course. We had planned on heading west for a twenty-four-hour voyage to Thailand. Our new course required a three-day voyage south across the Strait of Malaysia. It was a long, meandering journey, but finally our seasick and weary group found land near Tunnaganu, Malaysia. We drew close to shore and hastily began to disembark.

In the excitement, I was accidentally pushed from the boat on the seaward side. I could not swim and began to struggle in the water. Everyone else could swim and gave no thought to my situation until I had disappeared under the water. I struggled to the surface and was near panic as I screamed for assistance. After passing through prison camp and sidestepping death so many times on the way back to my loved ones, I refused to die by drowning so close to my journey's end. Finally, my cries of distress and my silent prayers were answered when a big plastic container was thrown to me. I held on tight as my rescuers pulled me to shore.

On shore, we were confronted by a group of school children. No one spoke Vietnamese, but I found one child who spoke English. With him translating for me, I informed them that we were refugees in search of help. I asked them to inform the authorities that we were here. In a moment, the deputy chief of police arrived, and I was relieved to learn that he spoke English. He asked me to accompany him back to the station. I was escorted to his very beautiful car. I was still dripping from my fall into the ocean and felt bad getting into this fine automobile while I was still wet. At the police station, I gave a complete report of what had happened.

The deputy chief said something I could hardly bear. He said we could not stay and that we would have to leave the next morning. He explained that because of his country's relationship with Vietnam, they could not take refugees from that country. If we stayed, we would be as badly off as we were in Vietnam. However, this was a good man who had compassion on us. He gave us sufficient food and fuel to reach the nearest refugee center, which was several days' journey by sea. We were allowed to stay unmolested overnight. He even sent a telegram to France for one of our party. All of this was done without payment. We learned that the previous night three boats similar to ours had been turned away and not allowed to land. How thankful I was that the Lord was still watching out for my friends and me!

BOAT OF VIETNAMESE REFUGEES ESCAPING FROM VIETNAM, 1975–87
(photograph courtesy George Reading Jr.)

BOAT OF VIETNAMESE REFUGEES ESCAPING FROM VIETNAM, 1975—87
(photograph courtesy George Reading Jr.)

When we got near the refugee camps, patrol boats came out and told us to go on to some other destination. They said the camps were full and we could not land. Refugees had become a burden to local governments. We obviously were not welcome. Finally, on October 11, 1977, we arrived in Mersing, West Malaysia, and we were permitted to come ashore. Mersing is a small town near Pulautanga Island, where many refugees were sheltered. At last, another obstacle was behind us.

When we arrived at Mersing, my desire was to contact the outside world from which I had been cut off for so long. I was alive and well but still needed help. I sent letters to Kan Watanabe, who headed the Church Translation Department in Japan, and to Elder Richard Bowman, the last missionary to leave Vietnam before it fell to the communists. We spent the night at Mersing and left the next day for the island where we were to report as refugees. We were accepted into the refugee center, and about one week later I received a telegram from Brother Watanabe stating that the Church had agreed to sponsor me and the others on the boat who had helped me escape. I was happy that I was able to fulfill my promise to them that I would try to help in this manner if they included me in their attempt. However, because many of my companions already had sponsors, only nine accepted Church sponsorship.

Although our excitement was great to be safely out of Vietnam, our little group found that we would be in the refugee camp for many months. Elder Gordon B. Hinckley, who was by now aware of my situation, contacted the Singapore mission president, Soren P. Cox, and suggested that I be contacted and helped with whatever assistance might be necessary. I was grateful to receive the clothes and books that were soon provided. As the clothes were too large for me, I gave them to my new friends who were also in need. Later I received more clothes, as well as two suitcases for my upcoming travels. For the time being, however, I wasn't going anywhere. Having braved the open seas and the weapons of my oppressors, I found myself buried in a mountain of red tape. Even with a ready sponsor and a waiting family and language skills, even with the help of the Church and friends in the United States, it still took me three months to be processed through refugee camp. Waiting under these circumstances was yet another experience designed to try men's souls.

In spite of my "freedom," I still felt very far from home. I received only one letter from my wife, but it was sufficient to warm my heart with sweet anticipation of what was to come. I knew that what separated us was mere time and distance, and not barbed wire or tyranny. Now it was all downhill; it was just a matter of time.

My time in refugee camp, despite my impatience to leave, seemed to have a purpose. When I was checking in with the Red Cross, the lady processing me recognized me as being one of the teachers at the language school in Saigon. I was soon appointed to be an assistant to the head representative for all the other refugees in the camp. I was thus able to assist many refugees as a spokesman for their concerns. When the head representative left the camp, I was selected to take his place.

Brother George Reading, a former Saigon Branch member, came from Singapore to see me at camp when he learned I was there. He stayed overnight with me in the camp, and we talked about the old days and rejoiced at my coming opportunity to live in peace and freedom with my family in America. I found out at that time that Brother Reading, who operated a shipping company, ordered the ship he left Saigon on at the time of the fall to remain just off the coast of Vietnam. There he oversaw the rescue at sea of a great many Vietnamese—as

GEORGE READING JR. IN SINGAPORE, SEPTEMBER 1984
(photograph courtesy Virgil N. Kovalenko)

many as would fit on his ship—as they fled the country in overloaded fishing boats. He was heartbroken and angry at the U.S. leaders over the outcome of the war and the resulting trials of the Saigon Saints and all the Vietnamese people. He had little desire at that time to return to America and made his home in Singapore. His unexpected visit, along with the concern and love he brought me, were very much appreciated. I cried tears of joy and thankfulness at the conclusion of his stay.

While I awaited my own release, I spent my time helping the refugees with their paperwork and other matters that required a language skill. I also presented their concerns to the officials who operated the camp. Since many refugees did not know English and would eventually settle in an English-speaking country, a school was started in which I served as a teacher. Just before I left the camp, the camp officials honored my service by naming the school after me. I was deeply touched and also amazed at my value as a person in the eyes of those in the refugee camp versus my worthlessness in the eyes of my captors in the reeducation camp. I left refugee camp with my self-worth fully restored.

At Kuala Lumpur, I spent my final ten days in medical checkups and final paperwork. In an effort to speed up my release, President Cox offered to buy my airplane ticket home, but the U.S. embassy rejected his offer. My case would be handled in the same manner as the others. Just in case, I was packed and ready to go at a moment's notice. I had nothing when I came to camp, but I accumulated through the kindness of others the two suitcases, clothes and gifts, money for my travel, and even a new suit. I felt very blessed. I also carefully packed away my dirty, greasy mechanic shirt as a memento of my river and ocean trip in October.

Finally, on January 15, 1978, I completed my processing and was allowed to begin my journey to my new home. I flew from Kuala Lumpur, Malaysia, to Hong Kong. This time I felt fortunate just to be with other passengers rather than having to hide below the floor with the luggage. I marveled at the speed at which we effortlessly floated over the same ocean that had been such a barrier to me for nearly three years now. For every mile closer I came to Lien and my children, I thanked my Heavenly Father.

In Hong Kong, I contacted Elder Jacob de Jager, who was kind enough to come to my hotel and visit me for several hours. During that time, he suddenly asked me if I would like to speak to my wife, Lien. I had not forgotten that I was free to communicate again, but I was not sure how to contact her.

Elder de Jager made the connection and handed me the phone. I stared at the receiver in my hand, hardly believing that Lien could be at the other end. Tears came to my eyes as, for the first time in three years, I heard the sound of her voice. We could barely speak through our tears of joy. I closed my moistened eyes as if I were dreaming. Then I was afraid to open them again. I feared that I might wake up and find myself in a reeducation camp in Vietnam. I feared that my hand might be grasping a cook's paddle and that my ears might be hearing the exaggerated wishes of a tormented mind. Only after soaking in her sweet voice to the depths of my soul and feeling of her love and spirit did I dare reopen my eyes and believe that her voice was real. My joy was overwhelming as I felt a great weight lift off my shoulders. Hopelessness and pity became foreign feelings once again. I laughed out loud. Freedom had never felt so good.

Once I had talked to Lien, my journey could not proceed fast enough to satisfy me. I traveled with fresh images of my dear wife and my precious children racing in my mind. My little girl, Linh, was only four months old when I had last seen her. Now she was walking and talking—in two languages—but did not yet know her father. My boys had also grown and changed greatly in the past three years. I had a lot of catching up to do.

From Hong Kong I flew to Tokyo. On the flight I felt out of place somehow. I looked up and down the aisles of the giant aircraft. I felt like dancing in the aisles and shouting for joy, but everyone else looked bored with the flight. Even reading was a joy to me. I read an onboard news magazine; it was like candy to my mind. I was hungry for accurate news. I was starved for new ideas. Prison camp had been like a vacuum in two ways. First, there was a vacuum of real information, and second, what knowledge and wisdom you did have in your head they tried to suck out. The news you were allowed to hear was propaganda; the thoughts you were authorized to think were force-fed by your captors. To think in a contrary way made you subject to punishment if deviation from the party line was detected. That is why reading a simple magazine was such a joy. I had not read a single uncensored word since my Bible was confiscated.

In Japan I was prevented from speaking to Brother Watanabe, but I could see him looking at me through the windows of the passengers' restricted area in the airport. I read his thoughts through his eyes and thanked him for helping to save my life and for being his brother's keeper. I felt I knew him well from my years on the translation committee and from his occasional visits to Vietnam, and I wished to embrace him and speak to him, but it was not to be at that time. Next, I flew on to Honolulu for a fuel stop and then to Los Angeles. When I arrived in Los Angeles, I was contacted by David Hoopes, the former presidential assistant who did so much for the Saigon Saints during the evacuation. Brother Hoopes arranged for me to speak on the phone to my wife once again. It was wonderful to hear her voice and report my journey's progress, but by now, her voice was not enough. I needed to see her. I told her that in a matter of hours, our ordeal would be over.

Still watching out for me, David Hoopes spoke to a representative of Western Airlines about my case. Thereafter, I received VIP, first-class treatment. Now I knew for sure that I was not in reeducation camp, dreaming. I could never have dreamed of being treated like an important person on a flight to Salt Lake City. I boarded the airplane and sat in my big, wide first-class chair. In contrast to my stay in the fishing hold of the small boat in which I escaped Vietnam, there was room for two of me in a single seat so large that my feet didn't reach the floor. I could stretch and turn at will without touching another soul. While flying across three states, I was waited on constantly and made to feel very important and special. I was well fed and provided with refreshing drinks. My friends in camp would love a clear 7-Up with ice and a nice sandwich like this, I thought, as I took a small bite out of a thick ham and cheese sandwich. I looked out the window at the ground and clouds below me. They were getting closer. I looked at the magnificent snow-covered mountains and the vast expanses of open land and tried to picture what my life in America would be like. I was awakened from my daydreams by the plane's captain announcing that we were cleared to land in Salt Lake City.

It was January 16, 1978. It was not only the beginning of a new year, but the beginning of a new life. I had now traveled halfway around the globe to reach my family. As we made our descent into Salt Lake City International Airport, I knew who to thank. My Father in Heaven had never seemed so real and so loving to me as at the culmination of my journey and my years of prayers. I sensed that His happiness on that day was as great as mine. It was because of the miracles He provided that I had survived my ordeal. His eye was upon me before I was baptized, and His hand had protected me through all my subsequent trials. It was only because of my faith in Heavenly Father that I did not quit many times along the way. As the wheels of the airplane touched down, I prayed for all those who were left behind and asked that God would open a way for me and others who had escaped to help them. I looked forward to being reunited with members of the Saigon Branch who were fortunate enough to have left Vietnam before the fall. I was anxious to hear their stories and learn of their lives in America. But as the aircraft approached the gate, there was only one thing upon which my heart and mind fixated—my family.

The aircraft came to a gentle stop at the gate. My heart pounded as I undid my seat belt and stood up to leave. I could see through the window as the Jetway rolled up to the aircraft; my heart beat even faster. My appreciation for my first-class seat increased as I realized I would be one of the first ones off the plane. Bursting with emotion, I walked off the airplane amid words of congratulations and encouragement from the crew. The anticipation was excruciating; my trembling legs couldn't move fast enough. I hurried down the long Jetway. It was cold. I continued down the corridor until I emerged inside the terminal. Suddenly, there she was! Lien was standing right before my eyes with my children. She was surrounded by her family and friends. My heart burst and my tears flowed freely. I rushed into her waiting arms. My children clung to our legs and waists as we embraced and kissed. She looked deeply into my eyes and embraced me again. "Thank God in heaven," she whispered into my ear, "you are home at last!"

My happiness knew no bounds as I basked in the love of my family for the first time in nearly three years. "Thank you, God," I repeated over and over again in my mind as I drank in their love and savored the sweetest moment of my life.

CHAPTER 12

Rebuilding Our Lives

Going "home" still seemed a misnomer to me. It took months for me to feel I belonged here. My wife and children had already adjusted to their new lives. By the time I arrived, my wife was used to doing things on her own. She was exceedingly happy that I had come home, but it took great patience on her part to suddenly turn over the mantle as head of the family to one so clueless as I was about the true depths of her own ordeal and her magnificent efforts to keep the family together. Over time, as I recounted the past three years to Lien and she reciprocated, I realized that she had been through a reeducation camp of her own. I was not the only one who had suffered during our long separation. She too had faced difficult days filled with difficult decisions.

While at the refugee camp at Camp Pendleton, my wife was offered a valuable sponsorship to live under the care of a wealthy LDS family in California. They promised her a good education and an abundant life for her and our children. The offer was restricted to just her and the children and did not include her mother and sisters and brothers, who were also in the camp. When Lien could not persuade the family to include the rest of her family or combine with another nearby family in the sponsorship, my wife sadly declined the offer. She and her family afterward received another offer of sponsorship from Brother Phil Flammer, a BYU professor in Provo, Utah. He was not wealthy but was willing to help them all. Their applications to leave the refugee camp were approved, and they moved to Provo. The BYU professor arranged for my family and my wife's family to live in two mobile homes at a trailer park in Provo. My wife's mother lived with my family and helped care for the little ones while my wife worked. Her siblings lived in the other trailer. My wife was discouraged by local Church leaders from applying for government welfare, as her fellow Saigon Saints in California were doing, and instead toiled long hours on her own to make a living. She was assisted through the bishop's storehouse with food and gratefully accepted the blessings it provided. My wife is a talented artist and had been told by some Americans in Saigon that she could make a good living selling her work in America. She gave up this idea because she had no art supplies and could not delay receiving the money she needed immediately to maintain her day-to-day life. She worked at the Barbizon Company as a seamstress by day, and she typed papers for BYU students at night.

All the while, Lien knew little or nothing of my condition or whether she would ever see me again, but she trusted in the message President Kimball left for her at the refugee camp. She bore her trials with patience and put her trust in the Lord. Although she was welcomed into the fellowship of her local ward, she faced discrimination and scorn from some people she did not know. They seemed to blame her personally for the loss of the war and the loss of American lives. As she went about her daily activities, she sometimes encountered ignorant people who uttered despicable epithets or treated her with cold indifference devoid of common decency and respect. These insults toward a woman of virtue and great worth in the eyes of God were tempered by the love and respect she received within the safe harbor of fellowship with the Saints.

It was difficult for Lien to adapt to a strange new culture. Simple tasks like washing clothes or cooking or shopping or simply getting from one place to another were new and challenging adventures. Even the change in climate, especially with the cold and snow of winter, required a major adjustment. While these were ordinary occurrences in an American's daily life, they were frightening to a newcomer.

The cultural gap was real and difficult to bridge. That is why I compare her trials in America to my trials at reeducation camp. In a way, both my communist captors and her American benefactors attempted to reeducate us by changing our way of life and teaching us a new way of living. At the same time, they discounted or discarded our former ways of doing things. Although her helpers were kind, while mine were brutal, the process of change was hard on both of us. Even as I suffered the effects of beriberi, Lien contracted tuberculosis, probably at the refugee camp, and required a regimen of prescribed medications for the next two years. I love my wife and honor her for bearing her burdens and her adjustments with courage and patience until I could return to her side and assume my share of the load.

Within a few days after I came to Utah, former Hong Kong mission president Jerry Wheat arranged for me to meet with President Gordon B. Hinckley, who was at that time a member of the First Presidency under President Spencer W. Kimball. While talking in the car before we went into the Church Office

Building for our appointment, President Wheat turned to me and asked, "Why did we have to go through all this, Tay? Why was the Church not allowed to stay in Vietnam?" I thought for a moment and then replied with what popped into my mind: "Because too many of my people were wicked. They were not worthy to have the gospel at that time."

President Wheat looked somewhat startled at my answer and then told me this story. After he had withdrawn the missionaries from Saigon and the communists took over the country, snuffing out the Saigon Branch in the process, he pondered day and night about why this was happening and to what degree he might be at fault. He prayed to understand God's will. One day, as he looked outside his office window at the mission home, he had a sudden and strong burst of inspiration. The Spirit told him to stop worrying about the matter and that everything was in God's hands. He received spiritual confirmation that he and Elder Hinckley and President Bradshaw had done the will of the Lord concerning missionary work in Saigon. Then he had heard the Spirit say in his mind the exact words I had just spoken: too many of the people were wicked, and they were not worthy to have the gospel at that time. He cried tears of gratitude as the Spirit reconfirmed to him all that had been revealed years ago at the mission home. It was our mutual belief that the missionary work that had begun in Vietnam would continue among those who had departed the country and that the gospel would return to Vietnam at some future time, when the people there were ready to receive it.

We met with President Hinckley for a half hour. He welcomed me home with tender words and a full heart. We also talked about the old days of the LDS servicemen's groups in Vietnam and the Saigon Branch. As our appointed time ended, President Hinckley invited us to eat lunch with him in the General Authorities' lunchroom. We happily accepted, and he soon introduced me to all of the General Authorities who were present in the lunchroom. Everyone was extremely nice to me and rejoiced with me in my safe return to my family. Later, on the way out of the building, I met President Kimball. Just as he had said, I was now reunited with my family. I never dreamed that such a day of fellowshipping with prophets and apostles would ever happen. My joy was full.

My children had adapted and grown splendidly in my absence. They had learned English, and the older ones were doing well in school. Little Linh did not remember me, of course, but soon warmed up to me. I was thrilled to merely stare at her and marvel at what a big girl she had become since I saw her as a baby at Tan Son Nhut Airport. Lien had remained faithful in the Church, and my children were taught the gospel in the home. My eldest son, Vu, was seven years old when I returned, and it was my privilege to baptize him the following year.

The trailer park where my wife and family lived was in the Sunset Second Ward. I joined my family in attending this ward and was warmly greeted by her new friends in the gospel. Eight months later we bought a house in the Provo Second Ward in the Provo South Stake. There were about thirty Vietnamese members in the Provo area, and I asked my stake president to help establish a Sunday School class for them. This was promptly accomplished, and a group of local Vietnamese Saints started meeting together at BYU for Sunday School. This may seem a simple thing, but how happy and amazed I was to be in the company of other Vietnamese Saints for the first time since the fall of Saigon. Furthermore, we met in freedom. We took no thought of being arrested for gathering together or being questioned about our motives. Many of us were former Saigon Branch members, but others were converted after they came to America. We wondered together about the fate of those still in Vietnam and prayed together for their safety and well-being. With only a trickle of letters from Vietnam to the outside world, and even less to America, there was little else we could do.

I was so happy the Lord had preserved me that I was willing to do whatever He asked of me in the future. Two or three months after we moved to the new ward, my faith was tested. It was very severely tested. My bishop called me to be an assistant scoutmaster. I cringed inside. I hated being outdoors! I hated camping! I had had enough camping to last a lifetime at the reeducation camp. I dreaded having to deal with young boys, all bigger than I, who were sassy and insolent by Vietnamese standards and would surely drive me crazy in short order. My mind was screaming, "There is no way I want to do this!" Even so, I heard my lips say, "I accept this calling." The very next day, the stake president called and asked me to meet with him. At our meeting a few days later, he called me to be on the stake high council, thus negating my assistant scoutmaster calling. Never has anyone so eagerly joined a high council. I was almost as relieved as I was the time I transferred from combat duty to the language school.

I was quiet and didn't say much in my new calling. I concentrated on learning my duties and getting a feel for the work being done. After two months, I raised my hand for the first time in high council meeting and asked a question: "Should not a high councilor be a high priest?" The stake president replied, "Yes, of course!" Then I confessed that I was not a high priest. Serving as branch president did not require ordination to the office of high priest, as is the case with a bishop.

The news somewhat shocked my stake president, not to mention the high council, and he immediately remedied the situation. I was called forward and sat down in a comfortable chair. The stake presidency and the eleven other members of the high council formed a circle, placing one hand on my head and the other on the shoulder of the man next to them, and the stake president ordained me to the office of high priest. I believe that I was among the first Vietnamese men to be so ordained.

Part of my sponsorship agreement to leave the refugee camp was that the Church certified I would be provided employment in Utah, and they promptly honored that stipulation. Fifteen days after I arrived in Utah, I was hired as a translator for the Church Translation Department. I was privileged to continue my work in translating gospel materials for the use of Vietnamese-speaking missionaries teaching the gospel to displaced refugees from my homeland. Thousands of former refugees were now living in close-knit communities in Canada, America, Australia, and France, and missionaries were being sent to them. I was originally hired by the Church as a private contractor. President Wheat, always looking out for my welfare, talked to the Church Personnel Department on my behalf and succeeded in changing my status to employee so that my family and I could be covered with medical insurance and other job benefits. I was also commuting from Provo in a carpool every day, and one day I was asked if I wanted to work at the Translation Department's Provo branch at BYU. These changes were great blessings to my family and me, and I was very thankful to President Wheat and Heavenly Father for bringing them about. I reviewed and finalized the completed translation of the Book of Mormon and Doctrine and Covenants. The original manuscripts saved prior to the fall of Saigon had been reviewed in Salt Lake City but not yet printed. I reviewed them again, and then I typed the translations into the computer. I also translated the temple ceremony, the *Gospel Principles* manual, and the priesthood, Primary, and Relief Society lesson manuals into Vietnamese. I was blessed by the Spirit in all of these efforts and knew the Lord had helped me. I had the continual reassurance that even though my country fell, the Vietnamese people had not been forgotten by the Lord. The gospel work was rolling forth, and Vietnamese far from Vietnam were hearing and accepting the gospel. I was thoroughly content doing translation work for the Church.

I was a high councilor for about six months when the stake president called me to be branch president over a newly formed Vietnamese branch in Provo. The Church owned a former seminary building in which we were to meet. We were thus able to hold meetings again in our native tongue in the fellowship of other Vietnamese Saints. I thought to myself that a remnant of the Saigon Saints finally had a chapel of their own. Sometimes our prayers are answered in a time and place and manner we could not have anticipated when we first offered the prayer. As I presided once again as branch president over a group of Saints now numbering about sixty—some from my former branch, but mainly new converts—I marveled at the tender mercies of the Lord. To be brought together in a free country in our own chapel was a dream come true.

A few months after I arrived in Utah, I received a letter from my friend Nguyen Cao Minh that brought word he had escaped Vietnam on a fishing boat and was in a refugee camp in Thailand. He was seeking sponsorship and assistance. I wept for joy upon receiving word of his escape. I contacted the Church authorities and told them of his plight. He soon had a

NGUYEN CAO MINH, 1984
(photograph courtesy Virgil N. Kovalenko)

sponsorship and passage to America. He came to Utah, and we had a happy reunion where we hugged and cried and shared our stories. When Dr. Nghia and I did not return from our ten-day reeducation camp as scheduled, Cao Minh became nervous about living at my house and pretending to be a draft dodger. He fled Saigon for the Mekong Delta, where he lived the life of a fisherman for three years, waiting his chance to escape. One day, he sailed out to fish and never went back. Our happiness at his success was tempered by the fact that we did not know anything about the Saints still in Vietnam. In the Mekong Delta, he was far removed from the Saigon Saints and had no new knowledge concerning them. The few letters from Vietnam that were approved by the censors had little useful information. My sister, Ba, had my address and wrote once every three or four months but had no knowledge of the Saigon Saints. I was relieved she was not reprimanded when I left Saigon. I sent her money when I could to help her and her family. The transfer of funds to Ba caused some angst in my own family, since we were also in financial difficulty most of the time and were not in a good position to share what little we had. Nevertheless, Ba and I had made a pact as children, which we still honored in that we tried to always take care of one another. She helped me get out of prison, so it was the least I could do to repay her.

I had another happy reunion within a year, this time with Dr. Nghia. He had been released from reeducation camp before me and attempted to slip out of Vietnam overland through China. The Chinese were having a border dispute with Vietnam at the time, and Dr. Nghia was arrested when he entered China and sent to another work camp. In the freedom of America, we laughed at his bad luck. I told him I must be the wiser because, even though he had a medical degree, he had to be reeducated twice. His medical skills were honored in China, and he was given better treatment than in Vietnam. He had provided medical services to the prisoners in work camps and was not always under close supervision like other prisoners. One day, he walked away from the camp and escaped to Macao. From there, he made his way to Hong Kong and eventually to America. Thus, within an eighteen-month period, the three of us who had once traveled together by bus to Ca Mau seeking a means of escape from Vietnam were all able to reach the distant shores of freedom we had so long sought. Dr. Nghia settled in Philadelphia, where he passed his medical exams and found work as a doctor in a large hospital.

In 1980 I took my family to the Provo Temple, and there my wife and I were sealed to one another, and our three children were sealed to us for time and all eternity. Of all the spiritual blessings that came to me, perhaps this was the sweetest and the longest in coming. I had anticipated this day since before I was even married. I had pictured Lien across the altar from me even as I helped translate the missionary discussions for her and her sisters. Through all my time in the reeducation camp, I had clung to the hope that this day would come and that I must persevere and survive my ordeal so that it could happen. When it actually did come, I was overcome with joy but was amazed with the ease and grace of the actual event, so far removed from my trials and my imprisonment. I could only bask in the Spirit and thank my Heavenly Father for allowing me to live long enough to do this work. Later, I was sealed to my parents, and I felt an assurance that they accepted the temple work done in their behalf.

My work with the Church Translation Department was completed after three years, and my employment there ended. This caused my family and me a great deal of financial stress as I tried to find other ways to support my family. One of my first attempts was rather comical. I had an LDS friend in the Provo area named David Garfield, who was an "idea man." He often dreamed up ways to become rich but needed someone else to manage the actual work. He hired me to work in his exercise equipment business as a manager. Due to my small size and low weight, it was obvious to anyone that I did not need or use the machine I was promoting. The very existence of such a machine was an enigma to me. In my former country, no one had enough food to get fat, and everyone worked so hard all day to maintain a living that seeking additional exercise was nonsense. I got a lifetime of exercise at reeducation camp, and I was still skinny from years of insufficient food and nourishment. I was too small and weak to properly demonstrate the machine's features. Still, I made an attempt to convince overweight Americans that using such a machine would be beneficial to them. The business closed after four years, and I once again sought other ways to earn a living.

I decided to open a gift shop with inexpensive items imported from Asia. I rented a store on Center Street in downtown Provo and sold a variety of things I thought Americans might like. They didn't. My store was a creeping failure, but I nursed it along for a few years. I tried to supplement my income from the store by selling life insurance for a while. Death was something I could relate to. Life insurance on my relatives would have been helpful to me on many occasions in my youth, but no one carried such insurance. I was not a very successful insurance man. Later, I sold vacuum cleaners, or to be more precise, I demonstrated vacuum cleaners that were for sale. I cleaned one room in each prospective customer's home for free as a demonstration of how well the machine worked. I cleaned many rooms but didn't sell many vacuum cleaners. Immensely discouraged, I wondered if I had what it took to make it in the land of plenty.

After the exercise business closed, David Garfield started another business building low-cost homes. When my store closed, he asked me to help manage his construction business. The timing wasn't very good. The hardest winter for many years dropped two feet of snow in the valley and brought construction work to a standstill. Then, it just kept snowing, thawing, and snowing some more. I organized our construction equipment into a snow removal business at schools and hospitals for the winter, but it was not enough to sustain the business. We had to lay off most of the employees. I was very discouraged.

I was in a pathetic financial condition, and I had a growing family to support. My two sons served Vietnamese-speaking Church missions. Vu went to San Jose, California, where many Vietnamese settled after the evacuation in 1975. Huy served in the Washington, D.C., area among both Vietnamese and Americans. For about one year, both were in the mission field at the same time, and the financial strain was heavy on the family finances.

The Lord had already blessed me so much and provided so many miracles for my benefit that I had restrained myself from asking for more. But in February 1993, with snow on the ground, bills stuffing the bill box, and wide-open spaces in the pantry, the level of my discouragement was such that I relented and poured out my heart once again to my Heavenly Father. I prayed earnestly that He might open a way for me to accomplish the purposes for which He had preserved my life. I prayed the same prayer many times over the course of the next few days. Heavenly Father, as usual, was ready and able to help me. From out of the blue, a man I did not know called me

TAY'S FAMILY TODAY
BACK: youngest daughter Linh; Tay; wife Lien; oldest son Vu
FRONT: second son Huy; grandson Tanner; granddaughter Taylin, daughter-in-law Kimberly
NOT PICTURED: son-in-law Mark Jolley; granddaughter Kaylie

(photo courtesy of The Van Nguyen)

and said that he had heard I was a good translator. He said he was calling on behalf of an agency of the United States government and asked me if I was interested in employment as a translator. I could barely retain my composure as I said, "Yes, I am interested in such work." He arranged for me to take a language skill test in Salt Lake City, where I also filled out an application for employment. This reminded me of my experience in the army when I had applied for a teaching position at the language school. Another door had been opened to me, and I would be sorely disappointed if I was not selected and allowed to enter. In the interim between my testing and receiving the results, I found out that over twenty-five others, some from my former language school in Vietnam, had applied for the same work but had failed the test. I was very scared at that point because I knew my English was not better than that of some of the others in that group. As I did in the army, I bided my time as best I could and anguished over the test results. Finally, word came back that I had passed! This was incredibly good news. My wife and family all celebrated with me. At the time we needed it most, I was finally assured of steady employment and benefits that would support and sustain my family. It was another miracle, and I thanked God for it. I was hired as a translator for the government agency and have been working in that capacity ever since. My wife also found work as a civil service employee for the state of Utah.

My daughter, Linh, followed her brothers' examples and accepted a mission call. She served a Spanish-speaking mission to New York City. All three of my children graduated from Brigham Young University. With talents inherited from their mother, they all earned degrees involving art. One is a fashion designer, one an industrial engineer, and one an art teacher. All who have married did so in the house of the Lord.

Now, I am a grandfather. I have done as the Lord desires for all His children in that I have joy in my posterity. Every dream I had for my life and my family has come true. Yes, I've had a few nightmares mixed in, but the Lord proved Himself a tender and merciful God.

When your heart is troubled, when you are feeling abandoned, when you have difficult trials, when your life is not as you know it should be, remain faithful. First and foremost, remember the Savior and the Atonement and that He overcame all things for you. Remember also my story and that of the Saigon Saints, the scattered flock. Although we had many difficult trials, the Lord blessed us and sustained us through them all. Everything worked out in the end. He can do the same for you. Praise be to God! Hosanna, hosanna to God and the Lamb!

EPILOGUE

Throughout my time as a political prisoner at Mr. Five's and in the subsequent years after I left Vietnam, my heart ached for the Saigon Saints who did not make their way to freedom. The communication embargo between Vietnam and the United States was successful, by and large, in preventing any word about that remnant of Saints from reaching America. Those who did escape after the fall of Saigon generally had little knowledge of others in the scattered flock. So it was with me. I only knew in my heart that the remnant of the branch left behind must be struggling. I reflected upon their predicament often, and even though I was helpless to do anything, I prayed for a way to help them. In time, a way was opened so that not only I but also many others could help those left behind.

The extent of their trials was brought to light seven years after the fall of Saigon when the restrictions on mail were eased and some letters trickled out. One of the first and most important letters arrived at Church headquarters in 1982 addressed simply: "V. Kovalenko, Church of the LDS (Mormon), Utah, USA." The letter was from Sister Xuan, Brother Thach's wife, and was sent to Virgil Kovalenko, an LDS Vietnam veteran who was formerly their home teacher. Someone at Church headquarters, not knowing who Brother Kovalenko was, looked in the local phone directory, found his name, and contacted him about the letter. Brother Kovalenko had been actively seeking information on this family ever since the end of the war and was overjoyed to know they were still alive. Cao Minh, who knew Brother Thach well, was called upon to translate his wife's letter and informed me of its arrival. Brother Thach was at that time in a reeducation camp, and his family was in desperate circumstances of poverty and bad health. Sister Xuan asked if Kovalenko remembered them and if he could help. The answer to both questions was a resounding yes!

The saga of Brother Kovalenko's efforts to help the Saigon Saints still in Vietnam is a book unto itself. I will only say here that Brother Kovalenko formed an organization called the Veterans' Association for Service Activities Abroad (VASAA), which brought together dozens of LDS servicemen who had served in Vietnam, along with scores of other interested veterans and Church members in a united effort to assist their brothers and sisters in need. I was elected vice president of this organization and did my part to help. My coauthor, David L. Hughes, served as an early editor of the organization's newsletter, *The Lost and Found*.

As a group, over the next eighteen years, we not only supplied critical food, clothing, money, and medicine but also successfully established regular contact with the Saints in Vietnam, helped them make contact with one another, and assisted many of the Saints to legally depart the country through the United Nations Orderly Departure Program. VASAA'S official slogan was "They are there, and they are ours!" It was suggested by Elder Marion D. Hanks in 1982, a short time after Sister Xuan's letter arrived.

That slogan became the guide for all that transpired to find and assist the Saigon Saints.

Thus we see that the Lord did not forget those Saints left behind in Vietnam, and He has not forgotten the Vietnamese people. The Saigon Branch was only the beginning of the spread of the gospel among the Vietnamese. Today there are over five thousand Vietnamese members worldwide, principally in the United States, France, Canada, England, and Australia. Most former Vietnamese wards and branches have been assimilated into regular geographic wards. The Vietnamese branches in Garden Grove and San Jose, California, are two notable exceptions. The gospel is now being taught where concentrations of displaced Vietnamese people settled after 1975 and where the Vietnamese populations continued to grow. Vietnamese-speaking missionaries are currently serving in Montreal, Toronto, Seattle, San Francisco, Los Angeles, San Jose, San Diego, New Orleans, Houston, New York City, and Washington, D.C. Someday, full-time missionaries will return to Vietnam. I look forward to that day.

Every Saigon Saint has a story. I only regret that this book cannot tell all of the wonderful stories of faith and courage that deserve to be told about the Vietnamese Saints and those who brought them the gospel. I will leave you with a brief update on some of the wonderful people mentioned in this book. All information is correct to the best of my knowledge. I apologize in advance for any unintentional errors or omissions.

Sister Vy

Sister Vy, the principal translator of the Book of Mormon into Vietnamese, lost her wealth in the communist takeover. A woman of refined manners and delicate nature, she could not abide the intrusive changes after Saigon fell and simply disappeared from the flock. After the fall of Saigon, she attempted to escape at least three times. Each time she was caught. She spent a brief time in jail. When released, she tried again. Finally she gave up, deciding she would never taste freedom. She moved eighty miles away from Saigon to Vung Tau and for the next ten years assumed the pretended identity of a solitary Buddhist nun, living the life of a hermit in a cave formerly occupied by tigers. She emerged from the tiger den for good in 1985 when faithful branch members finally found her and brought her back to Saigon.

The first meeting of the reconstituted Saigon Saints after the fall of Saigon was held in a public park on Christmas Day 1985, Sister Vy's birthday. Under the guise of a birthday party, the Saigon Saints partook of the sacrament together for the first time in over ten years. They also met together in December 1987. Sister Vy was provided with enough funds to pay her back taxes to the government, a dispute that was blocking her exodus, and then she was approved to migrate to Canada.

In March 1988 she came to Salt Lake City to attend general conference. She met with President Hinckley and Elder Hanks and spoke at a VASAA reunion. At conference, she sat on the first row with me and Cao Minh as special guests of the First Presidency. Forty-six General Authorities came from their seats to greet us. She also went through the Salt Lake Temple for her own endowments during her visit. In 1997 Sister Vy returned to Salt Lake and presented President Hinckley with a book containing seventeen generations of her royal lineage.

One of her sons lives in southern California. He flies helicopters for offshore oil rigs. She lived in Long Beach, California, for many years, where she attended the Los Angeles Temple

SACRAMENT MEETING DISGUISED AS A BIRTHDAY PARTY FOR SISTER VY
IN SAIGON PARK, DECEMBER 25, 1985
(photograph courtesy Nguyen Ngoc Thach)

SACRAMENT MEETING OF SAIGON SAINTS, DECEMBER 28, 1987
(photograph courtesy Nguyen Ngoc Thach)

SISTER VY AND SISTER TRAN THI XUAN IN PARK IN SAIGON, APRIL 1987
(photograph courtesy Virgil N. Kovalenko)

VIETNAMESE PIONEERS
SISTER VY AND NGUYEN CAO MINH ON TEMPLE SQUARE, APRIL 1988
(photograph courtesy Ruth C. Kovalenko)

SAIGON SAINTS AT BROTHER THACH'S HOUSE OUTSIDE SAIGON, ABOUT 1987
(photograph courtesy Nguyen Ngoc Thach)

SISTER VY PRESENTS COPY OF ROYAL GENEALOGY TO
LDS PRESIDENT GORDON B. HINCKLEY, JANUARY 7, 1997
(photograph courtesy Cynthia Brooks)

regularly. In 2002 she moved back to Canada to live with her daughter. She died there on November 17, 2003.

Nguyen Cao Minh

Cao Minh, the first Vietnamese elder, moved from Saigon to the Mekong Delta in 1975, where he took up the life of a fisherman. Three years later, he took out his fishing boat and kept on going all the way to Thailand. He obtained sponsorship through the Church and came to Utah. He lived in Utah for a few years, where he once again served as a branch president in a Vietnamese branch. Cao Minh moved to California, where he has worked for many years for the emergency services of the city of Los Angeles. He still resides there and has remained faithful in the gospel.

Le Van Kha

Brother Kha, second counselor in the Saigon Branch at the time of the fall, continued his work as a hospital administrative manager until 1990. After faithfully partaking of the sacrament by himself for over ten years, he attended the "birthday" meeting of the Saigon Saints in 1985 and was privileged and overjoyed to bless and pass the sacrament to all those present. His letters to America were long, filled with poignant scriptural phrases in the language of Paul the Apostle. He wrote them in English and constantly praised the Lord for not forgetting the Saigon Saints. He immigrated to the United States in 1990 and settled in Virginia with his wife's relatives. After years of being the only Church member in his family, he was privileged to see his wife and one of his sons finally accept baptism. At this writing he is in frail health.

Brother Thach

It was Brother Thach's wife, Xuan, who sent a plea for help to their former home teacher. This set off a series of events that culminated in the reunification of the Saigon Branch members still in Vietnam.

Though lacking an organized branch, Brother Thach was given a verbal and written commission from the Asia Area president to be the presiding elder in Vietnam. He was provided Church lesson manuals that he discreetly circulated page by page among the rest of the group. Brother Thach was imprisoned three separate times and was tortured and abused by his captors. Even after he was released, like other former prisoners, he was denied the privileges of citizenship and was not allowed to work for others, and his children were not allowed to attend public school. He remained faithful to his testimony through all his trials and unspeakable deprivations. VASAA provided Brother Thach with a cyclo-taxi with which he pedaled tourists and citizens around Saigon and was thus able to earn a living.

Brother Thach, his wife, and four of their nine children immigrated to America. He arrived May 8, 1996. He currently lives with his youngest daughter, Hanh, in Rose Park, a community in Salt Lake City. Another married daughter, Nga, lives with her family in Salt Lake City. Sister Xuan returned to Vietnam to visit her children and grandchildren who could not immigrate. While there, she died from complications from a long-standing illness. She is buried near her two eldest children, who died in early childhood. Thach, Xuan, and Hanh were sealed in the Jordan River Temple by Elder Marion D. Hanks. This fulfilled a promise made to them by LDS servicemen of the Bien Hoa Group in 1971.

DOAN VIET LIEU

The Doan family, with Colonel Lieu in his son's pajamas, escaped Saigon in the helicopter evacuation. As recorded in his daughter's journal, the family was reunited in Guam. From there, they went to Camp Pendleton. They settled in California and pulled together as a family. At first, they all worked in the vast vegetable fields near Salinas and pooled their resources until they had a firm grasp on the American dream. The parents, highly educated in Vietnam, eventually found good jobs in America. Their children excelled in school and became productive citizens, with at least one doctor and two pharmacists among them. Their success was duplicated by many other LDS Vietnamese families, who arrived with nothing but eventually prospered in their new home.

TRAN VAN LONG

Brother Long, one of the first Vietnamese elders, and his family suffered many hardships after the fall. His daughter, Anh, was caught trying to escape the country and was imprisoned in the North for many years. When contact was reestablished with the remnant of the Saigon Saints still in Vietnam, it was Brother Long (and later Brother Thach, when he was released from prison camp) who searched them out and told them of the new organization formed to help them. Brother Long acted as a "counselor" to Brother Thach during the years 1985–1991. Brother Long, his wife, his daughter Anh, and his son Dung left Vietnam, while the rest of his family remained.

Brother Long and his wife and these two of their children arrived in San Francisco April 8, 1991. Brother Long became disillusioned when success in America was slow in coming in San Francisco. He moved his family to San Jose and joined the Vietnamese branch there. Brother Long has since passed away.

Dr. Nghia

Dr. Nghia, who had to be reeducated twice, once in a Vietnamese prison camp and again by the Chinese, settled in Blairsville, Pennsylvania. He married and has a family. He works as a doctor in a large Philadelphia hospital and remains faithful in the gospel.

Ba

My sister and her husband have eight children. Those who are still at home live in the same home Ba and I built before I joined the Church. Ba and her family still operate a produce business in the market where Ba and I started the business as orphans. We write to each other regularly. On the occasion of Tet each year, I send a little money, along with my love, in remembrance of our frequently validated childhood vow to always help one another.

David Hoopes

Brother Hoopes, who was so helpful during the evacuation of the Saints, remained a special assistant to the president at the White House until 1977. He settled in California, where he worked as a financial consultant. Now retired, he served as a mission president in Chile and is currently president of the Caracas Venezuela Temple. His wife, Diane Tuttle Hoopes, serves as matron.

President William S. Bradshaw

President Bradshaw returned to his home in Orem, Utah, and resumed his career as a professor at Brigham Young University.

President Jerry Wheat

President Wheat returned to Hong Kong to preside over the Hong Kong Temple. He succeeded W. Brent Hardy, another faithful Saint who presided first over the Hong Kong Mission and then over the Hong Kong Temple.

Elder Richard T. Bowman

Brother Bowman lives with his family in Plano, Texas, where he is a renowned medical doctor.

Elder Dee Oviatt

Brother Oviatt lives with his family in Urbandale, Iowa. He was very helpful in providing details in this book about the full-time missionaries in Saigon.

Elder James L. Christensen

Brother Christensen lives with his wife, Charlene, and family in Draper, Utah. He is a partner in a Salt Lake City law firm.

Elder Richard C. Holloman

Brother Holloman retired as a pilot from the U.S. Air Force. He worked for the U.S. government for many years as an Asian expert. He currently works as a consultant on special projects.

Elder David T. Posey

Brother Posey lives in Sandy, Utah. He is a partner in a CPA firm in Salt Lake City.

Elder Colin Van Orman

Elder Van Orman returned to his home in Calgary, Alberta, Canada. He finished medical school and became a pediatric neurologist. He immigrated to Salt Lake City, where he works at Primary Children's Hospital. He and his family live in Bountiful, Utah.

The Saigon Branch

There is a small branch of the Church in Saigon today, although the Vietnamese and foreign members are required to meet separately. The current branch president is Joel Guttormsen, who is working in Vietnam for a large oil company. The mission president in Cambodia is also responsible for Laos and Vietnam. Missionaries in Cambodia have baptized over a thousand new members in the past two years. It is only a matter of time before the work of the Lord once again takes hold in Vietnam and the gospel is preached and accepted in my homeland. Of this I am certain.

I thank my Heavenly Father for all of the blessings He has poured out on faithful Saints everywhere, in the past, in the present, and in the future. I bear witness of His tender mercies and recognize His hand in all things that are good. I am most pleased and appreciative that my story and that of the Saigon Saints has finally been told. I hope your testimony, faith, and inspiration were somehow lifted within these pages. May God be with you till we meet again.

TIMELINE OF THE SAIGON SAINTS

MID–LATE 1950s: A few LDS civilians and diplomats work in Vietnam. Engineer David Allan Firmage and his wife, Margaret, and their children arrive in Saigon, July 1957, the only LDS members in the country.

JULY 8, 1959: Major Dale Buis and Sergeant Chester Ovnand are killed by guerrillas at Bien Hoa, the first Americans to die in what would be called the Vietnam Era.

OCTOBER 1961: President John F. Kennedy decides to provide South Vietnamese president Diem more equipment and advisers. Top aides recommend combat troop intervention; Kennedy disagrees.

FEBRUARY 6, 1962: American Military Assistance Command is formed in Saigon. By mid-1962 American advisers are increased from 700 to 12,000. Among them are several LDS members, including families of military members: Maurice Lee, USAF; Cecil Cavender, USN, and family; Loring Bruce Bean, USAF, and his wife, Pat; and Reed Prestgard. They form the first LDS branch and perform the first baptism of record: John Talbot Mulleneaux, Captain, USAF, on November 3, 1962, in a font made of a rubber water tank (see *Church News,* November 24, 1962).

AUGUST 8, 1963:	Nguyen Cao Minh is baptized and ordained in Biloxi, Mississippi, while going through intensive communications training at Keesler Air Force Base. Cao Minh is the first Vietnamese man to receive the Melchizedek Priesthood.
1963:	Three Vietnamese girls are baptized, the first of their in-country population.
NOVEMBER 2, 1963:	Diem and Nhu are murdered following a coup staged by Vietnamese generals.
END OF 1963:	Lyndon Johnson has sent in 15,000 American military advisers and provided more than $500 million in aid during the year.
OCTOBER 1964:	China explodes its first atomic bomb.
JULY 25, 1965:	Eleven men approved to become LDS chaplains meet with Elder Boyd K. Packer due to more Americans being sent to Vietnam.
AUGUST 1965:	Robert Lewis and his wife, Carol Taylor Lewis, arrive in Saigon. Sister Lewis is called to be the first Relief Society president in the Saigon Branch. They remain in Vietnam until 1969. Brother Lewis, a civilian architect, serves in the branch presidency briefly.
DECEMBER 1965:	American military strength increases to 200,000. Bombing of North Vietnam continues throughout the year.

1965:	LDS group leader Ray Young arranges for construction of an LDS chapel at Bien Hoa Air Base, northeast of Saigon. The chapel, built without Church funds, becomes a center of refuge for LDS personnel flowing through Bien Hoa for ten years.
1965–1971:	General Authorities visit LDS servicemen throughout the Republic of Vietnam; among them: Ezra Taft Benson, Bruce R. McConkie, A. Theodore Tuttle, Marion D. Hanks, and Gordon B. Hinckley.
April 30, 1966:	Tran Van Long and his wife, Nguyen Ngoc Dung, are baptized in Saigon.
August 1966:	Henry Kissinger and North Vietnamese negotiator Xuan Thuy meet secretly in Paris to start discussions for ending the war.
September 3, 1966:	The Van Nguyen is baptized.
October 1966:	Elders Marion D. Hanks and Gordon B. Hinckley hold conferences throughout Vietnam. In Saigon, Elder Hinckley dedicates the land for the preaching of the gospel. By this time, South Vietnam is divided into three major districts, with more than twenty LDS servicemen's groups scattered throughout the land.
December 1966:	American military strength reaches 400,000.

AUGUST 25, 1967:	Cong Ton Nu Tuong-Vy, descendant of Vietnamese royalty, is baptized in Saigon.
DECEMBER 1967:	American troop strength is listed at 500,000.
JANUARY 23, 1968:	USS *Pueblo* is seized by North Koreans.
JANUARY 31, 1968:	The Tet Offensive begins, with North Vietnamese and Viet Cong attacking many cities and towns.
1969–1970:	More than 1.5 million men under arms serve in Vietnam since build-up.
FEBRUARY 20, 1970:	Nguyen Ngoc Thach is baptized at Bien Hoa Air Base.
FEBRUARY 20, 1970:	Kissinger meets secretly in Paris with Le Duc Tho.
SEPTEMBER 14, 1970:	Tran Thi Xuan and two daughters and the family of Brother Thach are baptized at Bien Hoa Air Base.
JULY 24, 1971:	Bien Hoa LDS members establish "Project Temple" to aid Brother Thach and his family to go one day to the temple to be sealed.
DECEMBER 1971:	American troop strength is decreased to 140,000. Nixon policy states that all American advisers are to end their projects as quickly as possible; advisers are reassigned as a result.

When Faith Endures 259

JANUARY 25, 1972: Nixon admits that Kissinger is secretly negotiating with the North Vietnamese. LDS groups begin to close with draw-down of troops. The Saigon Branch is staffed by Vietnamese members.

JANUARY 20, 1973: Le My Lien, Brother The's wife, is baptized in Saigon.

JANUARY 23, 1973: Kissinger and Le Duc Tho sign a final cease-fire agreement.

MARCH 1973: The last American combat troops depart Vietnam. The LDS Group at Bien Hoa meets for the last time, and keys to the chapel are given to Brother Nguyen Ngoc Thach. He and his family continue to meet at the chapel until transferred to Can Tho. Brother Thach locks the chapel.

APRIL 1, 1973: American POWs are released from Hanoi; among them are at least three LDS pilots (Jay Hess, Larry Chesley, and Jay Jensen). LDS member and USAF officer Al Hansen (later VASAA historian) coordinates flights to retrieve POWs from Hanoi to Clark Air Force Base, Philippines.

APRIL 6, 1973: Hong Kong Mission president William Bradshaw brings the first four full-time missionaries to Saigon: James L. Christensen, Richard C. Holloman, Colin Van Orman, and David T. Posey. They begin studying Vietnamese with Sister Vy.

APRIL 8, 1973:	The Van Nguyen is set apart as president of the Saigon Branch.
JANUARY 1974:	War begins again between North and South Vietnamese forces. The only U.S. military presence is the Marine Guard unit at the embassy in Saigon.
APRIL 1975:	North Vietnamese conquer the South. Fierce fighting at Bien Hoa destroys the LDS chapel. Frantic efforts by LDS Branch president The results in the evacuation list approved by the White House (influenced by LDS members Roger Shields and David C. Hoopes, son-in-law of A. Theodore Tuttle). LDS member of the embassy staff Melvin Madsen assists as many branch members as possible to board evacuation flights. He boards the last plane but sadly leaves many behind, including President The.
MAY 1975–MAY 1985:	Most Vietnamese priesthood holders still in Vietnam serve lengthy prison terms.
1977:	The Van Nguyen escapes and makes his way to Hong Kong. LDS leaders send him on to Provo to be reunited with his family.
12 MAY 1975:	SS *Mayaguez,* a U.S. Merchant Marine ship, is seized by Cambodian communists in the Gulf of Siam. Thirty-eight Marines die rescuing thirty-nine seamen.

1979–1989:	Thousands of Vietnamese, including LDS members, flee via flimsy fishing boats. This leads to the development of a United Nations program known as the Orderly Departure Program (ODP), with UN negotiating between Vietnam and United States. ODP allows relatives to leave legally for reunification with families located abroad. Qualifications are extremely difficult.
MARCH 1982:	A letter arrives at Church headquarters from Sister Tran Thi Xuan, wife of Brother Thach. He is in prison for the third time. The letter leads to formation of VASAA by LDS veterans. VASAA develops experience in ODP.
SEPTEMBER 1984:	VASAA president Virgil N. Kovalenko meets with the Vietnamese ambassador in private quarters at the Vietnamese embassy in Bangkok, Thailand. Talks include possible exchange programs and methods for LDS members to either hold religious services in Vietnam or emigrate via ODP.
APRIL 1985:	The first VASAA representative meets with LDS members in Saigon.
FALL 1985:	Sister Cong Ton Nu Truong-Vy is found living in a cave above Vung Tao.
25 DECEMBER 1985:	LDS Saigon Branch members meet for the first time in ten years and hold a sacrament meeting disguised as a party. Sister Vy attends.

APRIL 1987:	VASAA president Virgil N. Kovalenko locates and meets with several LDS members in and around Saigon. The Asia Area presidency authorizes reestablishment of the branch if it can be done in safety. Events preclude successful reestablishment.
JANUARY–FEBRUARY 1988:	VASAA officers visit members again in Saigon and visit LDS members in a refugee camp in Thailand.
MARCH–APRIL 1988:	Sister Vy, who emigrated from Vietnam to Toronto, Canada, visits Salt Lake City to attend general conference. She meets President Hinckley and Elder Hanks and sits with The Van Nguyen and Nguyen Cao Minh on the front row of the Tabernacle during the opening session.
MAY 1989:	Four VASAA officials visit Vietnam. They deliver medical, educational, and humanitarian supplies to hospitals, clinics, and schools; hold sacrament meeting with Dao Thanh Que, who had been a prisoner for over ten years; and give priesthood blessings to Brother Thach, Sister Xuan, and two of their sons, Quoc and Vu.
MARCH 23, 1991:	Nguyen Hai Chau and family arrive in California.
APRIL 8, 1991:	Tran Van Long, his wife, and their two children arrive in San Francisco through VASAA help.

MAY 8, 1996:	Brother Thach, his wife, and their daughter Hanh arrive in Salt Lake City.
MAY 16, 1996:	Brother Dao Thanh Que and family arrive in San Jose, California.
OCTOBER 26, 1996:	Bien Hoa veterans and spouses gather at Jordan River Temple to witness Brother Thach's family sealing by Elder Marion D. Hanks as fulfillment of his July 1971 promise.
JANUARY 7, 1997:	Sister Vy presents a volume of Vietnamese genealogy to President Hinckley. It contains the royal lineage of the Nguyen dynasty, which goes back to A.D. 950.
NOVEMBER 17, 2003:	Sister Vy dies at her daughter's home in Toronto, Canada, forty days before her eightieth birthday.

HISTORICAL NOTE

The Vietnamese government lists more than 1.5 million of its people as killed in action during the war and over 300,000 as missing in action, prisoners of war, or unaccounted for.

Considering that over 1.5 million Allied troops served in Vietnam and assuming the accuracy of the prediction of 1 percent being LDS, then approximately 15,000 Mormons went through Vietnam during the war. This would include military in uniform, civilians at the embassy and consulate staffs, civilian aid workers and civil engineers, and repairmen from many logistical bases in the U.S., as well as Australians, British, New Zealanders, and Koreans who were members.

According to the Saigon Branch records, which VASAA found after they were lost for more than fifteen years, there were about two hundred members. In the flood of evacuation flights and boat people from 1975 to 1976, approximately thirty million Vietnamese were able to flee Vietnam. The rest were stuck. After VASAA began its work, twenty-three LDS families still in Vietnam were found, and members of sixteen of those families were assisted to leave between 1983 and 1997.